THIS BOOK BELONGS TO:

....

PRESENTED BY:

....

DATE:

....

CAUTION: DANGEROUS DEVOTIONS

JACKIE PERSEGHETTI

Chariot Victor Publishing
A Division of Cook Communications

Chariot Victor Publishing,
a division of Cook Communications, Colorado Springs, Colorado 80918
Cook Communications, Paris, Ontario
Kingsway Communications, Eastbourne, England

CAUTION: DANGEROUS DEVOTIONS

Cover and book design by Paetzold Design, Batavia, Illinois

First Printing, 1995
Printed in United States of America
02   9 8

ISBN 0-78140-250-6

DEDICATION

for Bethany and Ben Perseghetti
—the very reason I began writing.
You two are deeply loved.
And for
other young believers everywhere,
who desire to grow in their walk with Jesus.

ACKNOWLEDGMENTS

First, to my beloved husband Doug, who is my best friend, partner, and supporter. Thank you for your words of wisdom, trying to stay up with me when I wrote late into the night, and for helping me to be all God wants me to be. I love you and couldn't have done this without you! Bethany, thank you for reading and giving helpful opinions on chapters hot off the press. Ben, thanks for your many homemade gifts of encouragement—they kept my heart singing.

To Dad and Mom, (Griffin and Perseghetti) thank you for what you have built into my life and for the love you have shown me. To my sister Michelle, your ideas on the hiker were great!

To my dear friends Nancy Korb, Pegi Tehan, and Mary Miller, thanks for the prayers, phone calls, and help in special ways. You'll never know all it meant to me. Also, thank you to friends at Faircreek Church, PPC, and Dayton Christian School. Your support and prayers were of great encouragement.

To all of the third to sixth graders at Dayton Christian School who answered my questions, thank you. You were a valuable resource, helping me understand needs and concerns kids your age are facing.

To my editor, Jeannie Harmon, Thanks! Your patience and understanding when I asked for yet another extension kept me from becoming discouraged.

Finally, the most important thank you of all belongs to God through whom all things are possible! To You alone Lord, be all the glory. . . .

TABLE OF CONTENTS

INTRODUCTION

CAUTION: DANGEROUS DEVOTIONS?!!

Well, it got your attention, didn't it? According to the dictionary, *dangerous* means "able or apt to do harm." Do not read this devotional unless you are prepared for an adventure. *Caution: Dangerous Devotions* might take you where you have never gone before. It could challenge you to learn something you didn't know. It could make you stop and think. It could cause you to grow!

As you journey through the New Testament, you will see how the Bible speaks to every area of your life. You won't walk away the same. So, if you think you can stand the danger, then journey on. . . . It's a great adventure!

It would be very foolish to begin a journey without the proper tools or map to understand where you are going. Here's a simple map of the New Testament:

The four Gospels—Matthew, Mark, Luke, and John—allow us to get to know Jesus and see His actions for ourselves. Each book allows us to see a special and unique side of Jesus.

Acts comes next. It is like a history lesson and shows us what happened as a result of what Jesus did.

The Epistles follow Acts. They are letters written to believers to explain why Jesus did what He did and to show us how we can live for Him.

Last but not least, is the Book of Revelation. It is like the final chapter of any book it tells us how everything is going to end up.

You may be thinking, *That's the map, but what are my tools?* Your tools are very simple. Begin with a receptive heart conditioned by prayer (a little preconditioning never hurts) to receive what the Lord wants to teach you and also your Bible. (Yes, I said your Bible!) Then look for these symbols to guide you through each devotion:

GETTING READY

tells you how to prepare for today's devotion.

THE JOURNEY

walks you through territory that will make you think.

CLIMBING ONWARD

gives you verses to look up in your Bible.

 CROSSROADS presents you with a question and two possible options from which to choose. Which one is the right answer?

 THINKING ON YOUR FEET encourages you to think for yourself and apply what you've learned.

 DANGER AHEAD warns you of things in the real world that could prove to be a stumbling block to your faith.

SKILL TIME encourages you to put your faith into action—it tells you something specific to do to make your faith grow.

So, blow the dust off your Bible, grab your gear, and let's begin the journey together. Oh, along the way, we might see a small compass. Like any compass, we need to read it to get our bearings and make sure we are on the right track. Well, enough of that! Are you ready to journey? Follow me!

GETTING YOUR BEARINGS:
THE BOOK OF MATTHEW

Each book of the Bible was written with a special purpose in mind. Matthew focuses on the Jewish people in Jesus' day who were familiar with Old Testament Scriptures and prophecies about a King who would come someday. Over and over Matthew shows how Jesus fulfills the Old Testament prophecies. There are twenty-nine quotes from the Old Testament in Matthew, and thirteen times we see the words "so it was fulfilled"! I don't know what you think, but this shows us that Jesus was no ordinary person.

The first seventeen verses of Matthew may seem quite boring, but they actually show how Jesus came from a royal line. God had it all planned down through the ages to the very last detail. As we journey through Matthew, notice how Jesus the King fulfills prophecy, receives God's stamp of approval, proves His strength of character, chooses people to follow Him, sets new standards with old rules, hands out royal invitations, and encourages us to examine and trust Him.

SAID AND DONE!

TAKEN FROM MATTHEW 1—2

GETTING READY

Just as you need to get yourself ready each morning before starting your day, so you need to ready your heart before you journey through God's Word. The best way to do this is to spend a few minutes in prayer. It doesn't need to be long—a simple sentence expressing a heartfelt desire will do. Each time you journey in God's Word, ask Him to open your eyes, and give Him permission to teach you.

THE JOURNEY

Have you ever been amazed when something you were told would happen actually happened? How about being told 300 different things about something—with all of them coming true exactly as said? Sounds impossible. Not in this case!

Perhaps Joseph wondered if this was all a bad dream. Over and over he rehearsed it in his mind. He loved Mary. Mary loved him. They were engaged to be married. They had never done anything to be ashamed of, yet Mary said she was pregnant! It just didn't make sense!

It didn't, at least, until the angel explained it to Joseph. Mary's baby was from the Holy Spirit and was one of a kind.

"You shall call His name Jesus, for He will save His people from their sins," the angel had instructed. That was what the angel had said, and yet the words had also been spoken hundreds of years earlier by the prophet Isaiah when he wrote, "The virgin shall bear a Son and they shall call His name Immanuel, meaning 'God with us.' "

When a census required Joseph and Mary to travel to Bethlehem, another prophecy was fulfilled. It stated that the Savior would be born in Bethlehem! These events were not merely coincidence!

On the night Jesus was born, angels joyfully announced the Savior's birth to shepherds, and told them to look for specific signs that would prove their message was true. When the shepherds came to the stable, they fell to their knees in worship. The baby fulfilled all the signs the angels had spoken of!

> **Prophecy is a message telling what God will do in the future. The prophecies concerning Jesus were made over 400 years before He came.**

The same night, wise men (who were advice givers to kings) noticed an unusual star in the sky. They knew from Scriptures what it meant and began their journey to find the newborn Savior. When they arrived in Jerusalem several months later and asked where this newborn king might be found, King Herod became jealous. In fits of anger, he ordered a decree that all baby boys age two and under be killed! As great weeping and wailing rang out in the land, more prophecy was being fulfilled.

Joseph was forewarned in a dream about Herod's decree and fled with his family to safety in the neighboring land of Egypt until King Herod died. Upon leaving Egypt, ("Out of Egypt did I call My Son," Hosea 11:1), you guessed it—another prophecy came to life.

Herod's son was now King, so Joseph took his family to a town called Nazareth. This fulfilled the prophecy "He shall be called a Nazarene!"

Time and again Jesus' life fulfilled prophecies about a Savior who would come and save people from their sins. There are more than 300 prophecies concerning Jesus. Jesus was no ordinary person!

CLIMBING ONWARD

Anything worth having usually requires a little effort. In Climbing Onward, you will need to use a little energy. (Don't panic!) Your Bible is all the equipment needed for guaranteed success. Just look up the verse and answer the simple question. This simple exercise builds spiritual muscles and makes you strong in the Lord.

Turn to Luke 22:67-71. This is one of Jesus' predictions about Himself. Here, Jesus is standing before the religious rulers just before dying on the cross. What does Jesus say about Himself? (Do you believe it?)

Skill Time

If you could sit down with Jesus and ask Him questions concerning things you might not understand about Him, what would you ask? Write these on an index card and tape it to the back inside cover of this devotional. When you have finished journeying through the New Testament, reread your questions and discover how many you are able to answer!

WOULD YOU BELIEVE IT?

TAKEN FROM MATTHEW 3

GETTING READY

Take a few minutes to prepare your heart. Ask God to speak to you from His Word.

THE JOURNEY

Have you ever seen and heard things that caught you by surprise? How did you respond? Perhaps that is the way the crowd responded.

"What's all this about?" someone whispered to another.

"I'm not quite sure," came the reply. "He sure looks weird, though! Let's get closer so we can hear."

"Repent for the kingdom of heaven is near!" cried out the raspy voice. It belonged to a man named John, who would later be known as John the Baptist. Everything about John was unusual. Instead of living in a tidy little house on the edge of town, John lived in the wilderness. Instead of eating normal food, John ate locusts and wild honey. As for John's clothes of camel's hair and a leather belt—well, they were practical, sturdy, and as plain–looking as the wilderness around him.

17

All of this was rather unusual. John the Baptist claimed to be God's messenger, yet he didn't live, talk, or look like a religious leader of his day! Instead, he was quite a different type of person!

People came from all over to hear John. A small crowd gathered by the water's edge. "Repent for the kingdom of God is at hand!" Those words seemed as strange as John's appearance. Repent meant to turn around; to stop doing or being one thing, and to start doing or being another! John was telling them to be converted in order to see heaven.

Doesn't this man know who he's talking to? they wondered. "We are Jews—the very descendants of Abraham! Surely, that qualifies us to be included in heaven!"

Locusts were insects often eaten by poor people. They provided a nutritious source of protein.

Others listened to John the Baptist's words and did as he instructed. As a result, John baptized them in a nearby river as a symbol that their hearts had been made right with God.

More and more people came to hear what John had to say. They recognized him as a prophet. Some who came were baptized; others scoffed. Among the scoffers were some of the religious leaders.

"A Jew being baptized is unheard of!" they sneered. "Baptism is done only for the non-Jewish who want to become one of us—God's chosen people. Why do I need to be baptized?"

From out of nowhere, a man approached John as he was busy baptizing people in the river. Looking up, John recognized Jesus—the very One whom he had been proclaiming! John couldn't believe it when Jesus stepped into the water. "Lord," John said, "I need to be baptized by You, yet You come to me?"

Jesus looked into John's eyes and spoke reassuringly, "Permit it at this time, for it is necessary to fulfill all righteousness."

By allowing Himself to be baptized, Jesus identified with all sinners, and gave His backing to John's message. "The kingdom of God is at hand . . . and He is now standing in your midst!"

As Jesus came up out of the water, the heavens split open and the

Spirit of God came down in the form of a dove and landed on Jesus. In that instant, God's voice spoke from heaven, "This is My beloved Son in whom I am well pleased!" God Himself spoke for all the world to hear, and when He did, He set His seal of approval on His Son, Jesus.

CLIMBING ONWARD

Look up Matthew 3: 1-17. (Go on, look it up!) Notice verse 17. How does God feel about Jesus?

DANGER AHEAD

There are many people who will have different opinions about Jesus. Some will scoff like the religious leaders, others will understand and believe. Don't be thrown off track by scoffers. God gave His divine approval on Jesus as His Son, and on no one else. There is no opinion that could be greater or matter more than God's.

WHAT IF I JUST...

TAKEN FROM MATTHEW 4

GETTING READY

Take a few minutes to prepare your heart. Ask God to speak to you through His Word today.

THE JOURNEY

When you have been promised something will be yours but you must wait to have it, how do you respond? Are you ever tempted by shortcuts or plans that will let you have it sooner?

At the baptism of Jesus, God spoke from a cloud, announcing to all that Jesus was His beloved Son. Soon after that Jesus went to the wilderness to spend time alone with God.

This wilderness was beautiful, but a barren wasteland. Between yellow sand and crumbling limestone there were twisted ridges running in all directions. The hills were mounds of dust with jagged rocks.

After forty days and forty nights, Jesus was weak, weary, and hungry. The stage was set for a series of testings He would undergo. Jesus was at His weakest, and Satan would attack at his strongest.

"Jesus," Satan said, "You look hungry. Obviously, God's not taking care of Your needs. If you're God's Son, why don't You turn these rocks into bread?"

How Jesus hungered! He could take the challenge, prove He was God's Son, and satisfy His hunger all at once.

"It is written," Jesus answered, "Man does not live on bread alone, but on every word that comes from the mouth of God." Jesus knew it was most important to have His needs met by God. He would not use His powers to selfishly meet His own needs.

Did you know Satan tempted Adam and Eve the same way? He appealed to their hunger, to personal gain, and to power and glory (Genesis 3:1-5). What Adam and Eve failed to do in the perfect surroundings of the Garden, Jesus did in a wasteland.

Satan took Jesus to the temple and stood Him on its highest point. "You say You are the Son of God; if You throw Yourself down from here, people will see You're unharmed. They will follow You!" Satan said, "Isn't it written that angels hold You up in their hands, protecting You from harm?"

Jesus knew He must call people to Himself in order to teach them about God, but He would not shock them into it. Jesus would not force God's hand to protect Him by doing something willfully foolish. Jesus said, "Do not put God to the test."

Satan tried one last attack to get Jesus to compromise. Perhaps Jesus could be tempted to take a shortcut—get the glory without the suffering of the cross. Satan showed Jesus the people and kingdoms of the world. "Bow down and worship me, and you can have it all—without cost!"

Jesus would not be tempted. He said, "It is written: Worship the Lord your God and serve Him only." Jesus would take no shortcuts. He had a mission, and He would complete it, no matter what the personal cost.

Satan had no choice but to leave. When he did, angels ministered to Jesus. Perhaps they brought Him food; certainly, they worshiped Him. Jesus had been pushed to the deepest possible levels of testing. Yet, He didn't go through these tests for His *own* good, He endured them to prove His character to us for *our* good.

CLIMBING ONWARD

In your own Bible, turn to Matthew 4:11. Specifically what two things happened after Jesus had endured the testing? Look at verses 4, 7, and 10. How did Jesus answer Satan's attacks?

THINKING on your FEET

How would you have reacted to these testings? How should you react to the temptations in your life?

THEM?!

TAKEN FROM MATTHEW 4

Getting Ready

Stop and pray, asking the Lord to teach your heart. Don't skip past this part, but stop and pray, asking the Lord to teach you heart. Checking in with God and giving Him permission to teach you is really important if you want to grow in your walk with the Lord and keep your journey exciting.

The Journey

When classmates choose teams, does it seem the most popular are chosen first? That's not how Jesus chooses. . . .

The flies were buzzing about as fish were being cleaned and nets hauled in. It seemed like any ordinary morning—that is, until something special happened.

Fishermen were all around, cleaning and repairing their nets. many spoke loudly and coarsely with one another, and some were plain crude. Being rough in speech and treating others with the same crudeness was just common behavior amongst these men. Hidden in this group, like a puzzle piece in a puzzle, were two men named Peter and Andrew. Being busy with the task at hand, they hardly noticed Jesus approaching. "Follow Me, and I will make you fishers of men," Jesus directly stated. Much to everyone's surprise, the two dropped their half-mended nets into the sand and followed Jesus.

Continuing on, Jesus saw two other fishermen who were sitting in a boat and mending nets with their father. They were James and John, sons of Zebedee. Because of their hot-headed tempers, James and John had been nicknamed "thunder." This, however, didn't seem to bother Jesus. He chose them anyway, and they followed.

One by one, Jesus was choosing His team. They weren't the most educated, nor were they necessarily the most talented or best liked. In fact, Jesus even chose a man named Matthew who was a tax collector—definitely not a wise move if you were trying to impress others. Peter was a loud-mouth who often said one thing and did another. Thomas had his own battles with unbelief, and Judas actually turned traitor! What was Jesus thinking? Didn't He know who and what He was getting?!

Tax—gatherers were considered traitors against their own people! They worked for the Roman government often charging higher taxes than required, secretly pocketing money for themselves!

Jesus knew everything about the men He was choosing, and yet He chose them anyway. Picking just the "most promising" was not something Jesus needed to do. Jesus was more interested in His disciples than He was in what they could do for Him. He accepted the disciples as they were, and He would help them become all they needed to be.

CLIMBING ONWARD

In your own Bible, look up Mark 3:14. The second half of the verse tells what Jesus planned for His team to do. What does it say?

Skill Time

Do you take time to "be with" Jesus? Find a quiet place and time where you can be alone for a few minutes. For the next seven days, make this your "meeting time and place" with Jesus. You might want to talk to Him about your troubles, spend time doing your devotions—or both! Whatever you decide, be consistent for the next seven days. Make the time to be with Him.

OUCH!

TAKEN FROM MATTHEW 5—6

GETTING READY

Be sure to pray, asking God to speak to your heart and help you understand His Word.

THE JOURNEY

Have you ever noticed how kids at school sometimes pretend to be something they're not? They do things because they hope to be noticed? It wasn't much different in Jesus' day.

Jesus began traveling throughout Galilee teaching in the synagogues and healing people. News about Him spread, and people began following Him. Seeing the crowd, Jesus led His disciples up a hill and sat down. The disciples knew this was serious. Often a teacher would teach standing or even pacing, but when he sat down it meant he was going to share something very important and close to his heart.

Jesus looked into the face of each of His disciples. "Oh, the blessedness of those who are poor in spirit—who know they have a need for God," He began, "for they shall be in God's Kingdom."

"Oh, the blessedness of those who are pure in heart—who are honest with themselves and God, for they shall see God." Jesus continued on, naming character qualities of those who would truly follow Him. As He was finishing, He noticed the crowds making their way up the hill, so He addressed them as well. There was much to be said to such a group.

Jesus looked into the faces of the crowd. Some came with sincerity, others with desires of gaining personal favors or healing. Some were curious and proud religious leaders who wanted to make an appearance. Whatever the reasons, Jesus knew the problem was the same. These people could not live up to God's standards of righteousness. This was something the religious leaders knew as well, and took it upon themselves to lower the standard of God's laws, by adding their own easier-to-keep rules. By obeying these added-on rules, a person could look like he was keeping the law on the outside, yet his heart was really far from God.

When the Jewish person prayed, he stood with arms stretched out, palms upward, and head bent down. It was a hard thing not to notice!

Jesus addressed this problem. "You have heard from the law of Moses that you shall not commit murder. However, if you look down on someone with contempt and call him a fool, you have committed murder in your heart, for you have set out to destroy that person."

Jesus continued, "You have heard this said to you, but I tell you something else." Jesus was giving new meaning to their old laws. Instead of just keeping them on the outside, Jesus challenged them concerning their heart attitudes. This was very uncomfortable!

Jesus continued, "Don't do things, hoping to be noticed by others. If you do, you will have no reward in heaven. When you give, give secretly. When you pray, pray to God. Don't pray using big words and long sentences to impress others, and don't stand in places to be noticed."

This was a big problem for many. Three times a day the people were called to prayer. Wherever a person was and no matter what he was doing, he must stop and pray. As a result, near the hour of prayer, some people purposefully journeyed into busy market streets. They wanted a large crowd to notice how religious they were when they stood praying.

Giving money to the poor, praying, and fasting (going without food for the day to show God how serious you were) were all thought of as things a righteous person did. As a result, people began doing them only to be seen by others. Those who were fasting would mess up their hair and clothes and even paint their faces white to make them look pale! Those who gave money waited for a crowd to walk by, then noisily and proudly threw their money into the bin.

Jesus was not fooled by people pretending to be one thing on the outside and something else on the inside. God's kingdom would not consist of those who were religious, but those who were right with God.

CLIMBING ONWARD

Turn to Matthew 5:20. What did Jesus say about a person's righteousness? Where must our righteousness come from?

DANGER AHEAD

In your life you will be tempted to do things only for a good show. Perhaps it might even be good things! Live truthfully, and you will never be labeled a hypocrite.

Uh-Oh...

TAKEN FROM MATTHEW 13

Getting Ready

Spend some time preparing your heart. Ask God to search your heart and show you what He wants you to learn. He may ask you to change. Be ready to follow His lead.

The Journey

When you look around church on Sunday, what do you see—Christians, right? Not necessarily. Have you ever heard the saying "Just because you're in the cookie jar, don't mean you're a cookie?"

The crowds gathered around. Seeing the large number, Jesus climbed into a nearby boat to speak to them. He knew this would help more people hear what He had to say, for sound carries best over water. The crowd stood quietly, waiting.

"A farmer went to sow his seed," Jesus began, "and as he scattered it, some fell on the path where birds ate it up. Some fell on rocky places where the soil was shallow, causing plants to spring up quickly, then die with the hot sun. Other seed fell among weeds that choked out the plants. Still other seed fell on good soil where it produced a great crop."

The crowd listened attentively. Being farmers, they knew what Jesus was talking about. Paths between the gardens were hard and packed down. Any seed accidently spilled there became an easy meal for birds.

They also knew that just two to three inches below beautiful soil, rocks might be found that could block a plant's roots from going deep down. If not rocks, weeds threatened to steal nourishment from the plants and choke them out. Yes, the crowd well understood Jesus' story.

Jesus continued. He explained that the types of soil were like types of heart attitudes people have toward God and His Word. Some people have hardened hearts (like the hardened path) and won't allow God's Word to sink into their lives. Others might have an interest, but when difficult times come (like the sun scorching the plant), they fall away and no longer want to follow Jesus or live for God. Yet another type of attitude is revealed in the person who starts living for God, but the things of the world crowd out their love for God. The last type of soil is the good kind; it represents the person who desires to live for God and listens to His Word. This person enjoys God's doing wonderful things in and through his or her life.

Jesus didn't stop there. Looking around at the crowd, He told another parable. He explained that God's kingdom (those who really believe and know God) was like a huge wheat field. The farmer planted wheat in it while an enemy secretly planted weeds.

The people listened eagerly. Tares were a type of weed that looked just like the wheat plant but were poisonous. By the time the grains developed enough to tell the plants apart, the roots of the tares would be tangled with the roots of the wheat plants. The farmer would then wait until harvest to separate the plants and destroy the tares.

Jesus told this parable as a description of people who are real followers of His and people who are pretend followers. The pretend followers would be allowed to be with the others (just like the wheat and the tares growing together), but in the end they would be separated and destroyed.

Jesus spoke these parables as a serious warning for all to examine their own hearts. What was their attitude toward God? Were they wheat or were they tares? Not all who claim to be Christians really are.

CLIMBING ONWARD

Read Matthew 13:49. Real Christians will be separated from pretend Christians. When did Jesus say this would happen?

Skill Time

Take a moment and think about Jesus' description of the soils. What type of soil is your heart today? If it's a little weedy or has a layer of rock underneath, tell God about it right now. Give Him permission to change your heart so it can be like the good type of soil.

BELIEVE IT

TAKEN FROM MATTHEW 11

GETTING READY

Take a few minutes to prepare your heart by asking God to help you understand what He wants you to learn.

THE JOURNEY

Have you ever hoped for something and then became disappointed when things weren't turning out the way you had expected?

John the Baptist paced back and forth in a tiny cell. It was dark and damp, almost like a pit. John had boldly spoken out to the governor of Galilee (Herod Antipas) and told him to repent of a wrong and evil thing. Herod Antipas became angered and wanted to get rid of John. He couldn't kill him outright, because John was considered a prophet. Killing him would cause an uprising. So Herod had John put in the dungeon of an old fortress. After a while, the governor planned to quietly execute John.

It had been one year since that time—a slow and painful year during which John had become a prisoner even to his own thoughts. John's only connection to the outside world were a few occasional visitors. These visitors had been his followers. Now they were following Jesus. They would come, bringing short reports to encourage John. John listened, but the more he heard, the more he became confused. Pretty soon, the confusion grew into nagging doubts.

John believed Jesus was "the One who is to come." He had based his whole life on this proclamation! He had seen the sky split open and the dove descend and rest upon Jesus' shoulder. He had heard God's voice from heaven, proclaiming to all that Jesus was God's Son. But wasn't the Messiah supposed to set up a new kingdom? Wasn't He going to judge people and put an end to all evil?

"One who is to come" is an Old Testament title for the promised Messiah. It was based on Psalm 40:7 and Psalm 118:26.

In the darkness of the cell, John the Baptist quietly questioned. From all the reports, Jesus was not squashing the enemies. The Roman Empire was evil, and Jesus did nothing to stop or overthrow it! Things were not going as John had expected. Could he have been mistaken about Jesus?

Desiring an answer, John sent some of his followers to ask Jesus a question that was burning in his heart: "Are You 'the One who is to come', or should we look for someone else?"

When Jesus heard this question, He gave a simple and direct answer to comfort John the Baptist. "Go and report to John what you hear and see: the blind receive their sight and the lame walk; the lepers are cleansed and the deaf hear; the dead are raised up, and the poor have the gospel preached to them."

These were all prophecies of what 'the One who is to come' would do. These were all things Jesus was doing. Then Jesus added, "Blessed is the person who does not fall away on account of Me; who doesn't lose heart when things aren't going as expected."

Jesus knew what He had come to do and He knew God's perfect plan and timing. John had been expecting everything to happen all at once, but that was not God's plan. John was instructed to examine Jesus' very life and actions and see how Jesus was fulfilling prophecies.

John must see the evidence and be patient, trust God and not doubt. Even though things weren't going as John expected, God was in control and knew the full picture. These were the encouraging words that were sent back to John the Baptist as he was beheaded by Herod Antipas.

Take a look at verse 6 of Matthew chapter 11 in your own Bible. What do you think Jesus meant by that statement?

When times get tough for you and you don't understand what God is doing, how will you respond? Will you remember His character and choose to trust Him, or will you doubt and lose all hope?

I'M NOT WEARING THAT!

TAKEN FROM MATTHEW 22

GETTING READY

Stop and pray, asking God to speak to your heart.

THE JOURNEY

Does it seem other kids always get invited to parties, but you do not? Do they brag about being invited, hinting they are better than you—that they deserve to be invited because they're cool (and you are not)?

The preparations were ready. Invitations had been sent. Guests were to arrive any minute.

But there was a slight problem—the invited guests decided not to attend the great party. Some were busy with other things, while others simply ignored the invitation.

As a result, the king hosting the party invited strangers. He sent his messengers into the streets to invite anyone they found, both good and bad. As these people were invited, the messengers handed them a clean robe like garment to wear to the party. This robe was a gift from the king.

Guests soon arrived and were enjoying the wonderful food. The party was beyond what they imagined! As the king came out to greet his guests, he noticed everyone wearing the clothes he had lovingly provided.

Then the king discovered one man who was not wearing the provided clothing. That man had entered the great party in his filthy, dirty clothes and had insulted the king.

"Friend," the king said, "how is it that you came in here not wearing what I provided for you?"

Wearing robes provided by the king purposely put guests on the same level with one another. No one could strut around claiming to be better than others!

The man was speechless. He had been foolish to think it would not matter. He looked at his clothes. They looked like filthy rags compared to the glistening white of the clothes others were wearing. He could have been properly dressed if only he would have put on the clothes that were given to him.

The man was taken from the party and sent out into the dark night. He was tied hand and foot so that he couldn't sneak back.

Having once been invited, he was rejected because he didn't make the right preparations for coming. He didn't wear what the king had provided.

Jesus told this parable to some religious leaders who thought they were better than others and were certain they deserved to go to heaven. In this parable, the king represents God who welcomes all into His heavenly kingdom. The only requirement is that they come dressed in the clean garments (the righteousness) that He provides. Anything else is unacceptable and will be rejected.

Look up this parable in your own Bible. It is found in Matthew 22. Look specifically at verse 12. What question did the king ask? How did the person respond?

Do you think God would ever ask you that question? Are you wearing the clothes of righteousness Jesus provided for you? If not, or if you are not sure, then read on! There's great news for you!

Skill Time

This is personal. It doesn't involve anyone else but you and God. Get alone in your thoughts for a minute and search your heart. Do you have a personal relationship with Jesus? Do you even know what that means?

Take a minute and turn to the last pages of Caution: Dangerous Devotions. There's a special message just for you.

GETTING YOUR BEARINGS:
THE BOOK OF MARK

As you journey through Mark, notice that it is the shortest of the four Gospels. It is a fast-moving book that shows many of Jesus' miracles. The Gospel of Mark has been called the book of action. Unlike Matthew, which shows Jesus as the promised Messiah-King fulfilling all prophecy, Mark shows us how Jesus was a servant. He proved who He was by what He did. Mark 10:45 says, "For even the Son of Man did not come to be served, but to serve, and to give his life as a ransom for many."

In Mark you will see Jesus' authority and ability to control what we can't. You will see Jesus' power over death, helping people regardless of who they are, and knowing all about the future. These are only a few of the many things found in the book of Mark. As you journey through Mark, see what else you can learn about Jesus.

WOW!

TAKEN FROM MARK 1

GETTING READY

Before you journey through today's subject, spend a few minutes talking to God. Ask Him to open your eyes to help you understand His Word.

THE JOURNEY

Ever notice how kids running for class president at school put up posters, trying to convince others that they are the best and most authoritative person for the job? Jesus didn't have to do that.

Who is this person?" one man whispered to another. "I have never heard someone teach quite like He does!"

The other man nodded. It was true. They were gathered together in the synagogue for the regular reading and proclaiming of the Scriptures. The president of the synagogue had called upon a guest speaker to read and teach the Scriptures. Any qualified man could do so, although scribes were usually chosen for this task since they worked so closely with the Scriptures.

Scribes had the duty of interpreting God's law. As a result of their job, many scribes came up with added-on rules. Whenever a scribe spoke, he was quick to quote others. Each sentence began with, "There is a teaching that . . . ," and often ended with the scribe quoting a famous Rabbi (Jewish teacher).

Jesus didn't bother to quote other authorities. He spoke as if He were the authority! Such teaching sounded fresh and new. It was a wonderful change from what the people were used to hearing.

Jesus was the guest speaker on this occasion when suddenly from the back of the room came a disturbance. A man who was possessed by an evil spirit cried out, "Jesus, what do you want with us? You haven't come to destroy us, have You?" The voice of a demon was speaking through the man and spoke for itself as well as for the other demons. They knew Jesus was the Messiah who had come to destroy Satan and his evil works. "We know who you are—the Holy One of God!" the demon said.

"Be quiet!" Jesus said sharply. He would not accept testimony from a demon. "Come out of him," Jesus sternly commanded the demon.

> There is a difference between the temple and a synagogue. The temple was used for worship and sacrifices, and there was only one. The temple was located in Jerusalem.
>
> A synagogue was used for teaching and instruction. Wherever at least ten Jewish families lived, by law there was to be a synagogue.

The demon had no power against Jesus. It let out a loud shriek and shook the man violently as it left him. The people who saw this stood speechless. They had never seen anything like this before! Yes, they'd seen demon-possessed people, and yes, they'd seen demons cast out, but never by just a simple command! Usually a special formula of words had to be said, and ceremonies done—and even then it wasn't always successful. Jesus healed this man with just four words! His power and authority were amazing!

Not only did Jesus teach with authority, but He also had authority over the demons! Because of this, news about Jesus spread quickly over the whole region of Galilee.

CLIMBING ONWARD

Look up Mark 1:24. What question did the demon ask of Jesus? What fact did the demon state about Jesus? The demons believed and knew about Christ's authority, but didn't trust.

Skill Time

What facts do you know about Jesus? Do they make a difference? Take a quiet moment to think about Jesus' power and authority. In what one area of your life could you believe and trust Jesus more? Pray and ask Him to help you in that area today.

I'M WITH HIM!

TAKEN FROM MARK 1

GETTING READY

Prepare your heart before God. Ask Him to teach you what He wants you to learn.

THE JOURNEY

Have you ever noticed how some people try to be the most popular? Not Jesus, although He had plenty of opportunities.

Crowds came from near and far. They had heard the news about Jesus' power, and learned Jesus was at the home of Peter and Andrew. Because it had been the Sabbath, they were not able to carry their sick to Jesus until now. (Carrying the sick would have been considered work. Working on the Sabbath was against the law.) Once the sun set and three stars shone, the Sabbath was officially over. As a result, the whole town had gathered at the door where Jesus was. Jesus lovingly healed their diseases and cast out demons.

The next morning while it was still dark, Jesus quietly slipped out to spend time with God in prayer. Peter and the disciples noticed Jesus was gone and went to look for Him. People were asking for Jesus, and a large crowd had gathered at the door. Jesus was becoming very popular and it seemed everyone wanted to see Him.

"Everyone is looking for You!" Peter said when they finally found Jesus. Peter felt quite proud to be associated with someone as popular as Jesus and was not ready for Jesus' reply.

"Let us leave here and go to the nearby villages so I can preach there also," Jesus stated.

Peter stood dumfounded. He saw no reason to leave when things were going so well. But Peter and the others obeyed Jesus and left Capernaum to travel throughout Galilee. Jesus continued to preach in the synagogues and cast out demons.

While they were traveling around Galilee, a man with leprosy came to Jesus. Leprosy was a terrible, incurable disease. At first a person would get spots on his body that turned into growths. The growths would grow and start to smell. Fingers, toes, hands, and other body parts that became infected would die, rot, and eventually fall off the body. Those who had this disease were considered unfit to live among healthy people. They were cast off to live in a place by themselves and had to wear black clothes to hide their twisted bodies. It was against the law for lepers to come near other people, and if they did, they were forced to shout "Unclean! Unclean!" so people would be warned to stay far away.

This man who had leprosy was so lonely and desperate, he came right up to Jesus, and fell on his knees. "If You are willing," the man begged, "You can make my leprosy go away, and make me clean."

Jesus looked at the man with compassion, then He did something unheard of. He reached out and touched the leper! "I am willing," Jesus said tenderly, "be clean!"

Immediately the leprosy left the man and he was cured! Jesus instructed him to tell no one, but to go show himself to the priest first. He was to be examined and to offer the sacrifices commanded by law in order to be considered clean (without leprosy).

Unfortunately, the man in his excitement disobeyed the Lord. Instead of doing what Jesus asked, the man went out and told everyone what had happened. Jesus had a reason for not wanting the leper to tell. He knew it would attract crowds for the wrong reasons and motives. Attracting crowds was not something Jesus came to do.

As a result of this man's disobedience, Jesus could no longer enter a town openly, but stayed out in the lonely places. Even then, crowds still came to Him from all over.

CLIMBING ONWARD

In your Bible, turn to the first chapter of Mark. Read verse 35. How did Jesus start His day? Where did He go? What did He do? How do you think that made a difference in the choices He made?

DANGER AHEAD

There will be times in your life when you will have to decide between the good and the best of opportunities. Watch the choices you make. Be sure to spend time talking to God in prayer and making sure you are on the right track. It has been said that a crowd of people doesn't always mean success, and "it is far better to be alone with God than in a crowd without Him!"

NOW WHAT?

TAKEN FROM MARK 4

GETTING READY

Stop and pray, asking God to speak to your heart.

THE JOURNEY

Have you ever had one of those days when nothing goes right for you and it seems nobody cares? Where is God when you really need Him, anyway? That was perhaps the very question on the minds of the disciples.

The wind was whipping up, and white caps formed on the usually calm lake. The disciples scanned the sky. It didn't look like a storm was brewing, but then looks were deceiving when it came to the Sea of Galilee. Bordered by mountains, the Sea of Galilee often had storms out of nowhere. As the wind squeezed down through the mountains, it would whip across the lake with a sudden burst. The once-smooth water would turn into violent waves, slapping and tossing boats around as if they were toys. As the winds began to increase so did the worries of the disciples.

"Let us go over to the other side," Jesus had told them before He'd climbed into the boat. He didn't say "Let's try to go to the other side," but simply, "Let's go." There was something final about the way Jesus had said that.

The disciples grabbed at the oars of the boat. They struggled against the mounting waves. Water spilled into their boat and waves tossed their boat from one side to the other. The disciples looked back and noticed Jesus was sleeping. He was riding in the seat of honor—a little seat in the back of the boat where a carpet and cushion were arranged. This was the seat in which any distinguished guest rode.

The disciples couldn't believe Jesus was sleeping through the storm. They continued to struggle with the oars until they could no longer control the boat. Half frustrated and fearful, they shook Jesus awake.

"Jesus," they panicked, "don't you even care that we might drown?" Perhaps some of them were muttering under their breaths "How come You're not there to help us when we need You?"

Jesus stood up in the boat. He had been waiting for them to come ask Him for help. Stretching out His hand He spoke three simple words, "Peace! Be still!"

Immediately the wind stopped and the water became calm. The disciples couldn't believe their eyes.

"Why were you so afraid?" Jesus questioned them. "Do you still not understand who I am? Do you still have no faith?"

It was true that the disciples had seen Jesus do many wonderful miracles. All of those pointed to His authority and power. All of them pointed out the fact that Jesus was not an ordinary person. If they truly understood who it was that was with them in the boat, they would not have been worried.

"Who is this with us?" they asked each other in wonder. "Even the wind and the waves obey Him!" The only One who could control nature was the very One who made it. The disciples looked at each other, terrified. Could it be possible?

CLIMBING ONWARD

According to your Bible, what were Jesus' exact words to the disciples in Mark 4:35. (Go on, look it up!) Notice Jesus didn't say to try to go, or go halfway and sink. What Jesus told them to do, Jesus would help them accomplish. Not only did Jesus have the power to help the disciples when they asked, but also He was with them through their circumstances even before they asked. The disciples needed to learn to trust Jesus' character.

Skill Time

Are you facing a difficult storm in your life? Kids at school making fun of you? Your grades aren't what they should be? Tell Jesus about it right now. Invite Him into your boat to help you through your particular storm, then thank Him (in advance) for His help!

YOU'RE TOO LATE

TAKEN FROM MARK 4

GETTING READY

Take a few minutes to quiet your thoughts. Tell God what is on your heart. Ask Him to help you understand what is on His.

THE JOURNEY

Does it frustrate you when you need someone's help and they take their time getting to you?

Jairus quickened his pace. By now he was practically running. *This is bad. This is really bad*, he worried to himself. His only child, a precious twelve-year-old daughter, was very ill. She lay in her bed at home dying. There was no time to lose.

Being the ruler of the synagogue, Jairus was well-respected in the community. He had a place of honor in society and had servants working for him. Somehow, none of that seemed important compared to the life of his daughter. Instead of sending servants, Jairus would go and find Jesus himself. *Perhaps Jesus can heal her,* Jairus said to himself.

Coming over the hill, Jairus saw a large crowd gathering around Jesus by the Sea of Galilee. "I found Him!" Jairus said with relief. Working his way through the crowd, Jairus fell at Jesus' feet and began pleading with Him. "Please, my daughter is dying. Come and put Your hands on her so she will be healed and live. Please, I beg you!"

To Jairus's delight, Jesus arose to follow him. Jairus's heart pounded with worry and excitement. His heart beat like a clock announcing precious seconds and minutes that couldn't be wasted. Would they get there in time? Jairus anxiously wondered.

The large crowd surrounding Jesus followed along. They were all crowding around Him, pushing and shoving to get close. It seemed everybody wanted something.

As they moved along, a woman slipped into the crowd. She had a bleeding problem that made her sick and labeled her unclean to others. She was lonely and desperate. Having tried all the doctor's remedies, she was now without money and feeling worse than ever. Jesus was her only hope.

Working her way through the crowd, the woman reached out and touched the corner of Jesus' cloak. Suddenly she felt her body being instantly healed! Just as suddenly Jesus stopped and asked who had touched Him in such a faith-filled way.

Jairus's heart sank. If they delayed any longer, his daughter would be dead. it would be too late! Jairus grew impatient. From the corner of the crowed, the woman stepped forward and told Jesus the whole truth.

"Go in peace," Jesus told her. "Your faith has healed you." The woman went on her way rejoicing. As she left, messengers came with news for Jairus.

"Jairus, don't trouble the Teacher any longer," they said. "Your daughter is dead." Jairus's sad eyes looked at Jesus.

Jesus ignored what the messengers said and spoke to Jairus, "Don't be afraid, Jairus. Just believe."

Jesus told the crowd to stay behind. Peter, James, and John were allowed to follow. When they reached Jairus's house they saw mourners weeping and wailing loudly. They had torn their clothes down the right side as was the custom to show they were mourning. Flute players were there, playing the common death and despair notes that blended with the loud cries and weeping. There was quite a commotion.

"Why all this mourning and wailing?" Jesus asked them. "The child is not dead but asleep." (Jesus said the child was asleep because her death at this time would not be permanent. He was going to raise her from the dead.)

The mourners laughed and scoffed at Jesus. After putting them all out, Jesus took the child's father and mother and the three disciples, and went into the child's room. Taking the little girl by the hand, He tenderly commanded, "Talitha koum!" (which means "Little girl, I say to you, get up!")

Mourners were often hired and paid money to weep and wail. Their loud wailing was an announcement to others that someone had died.

Immediately she stood up and walked around! The color had come back to her face, and life had come back to her body! The small group in the bedroom stood speechless. Jesus gave them strict orders not to let anyone know about this, and told them to give the girl something to eat.

CLIMBING ONWARD

What did Jesus tell the synagogue official in Mark 5:36? (Look it up in your Bible.) With Jesus, nothing is ever too late, or beyond His ability to change. That was something Jairus learned first-hand.

THINKING on your FEET

What will you do the next time things don't seem to happen quick enough, or aren't going the way you want them to go?

EVEN SO . . .

TAKEN FROM MARK 7

GETTING READY

Take a few minutes to prepare your heart. Ask God to quiet your thoughts and help you learn from His Word today.

THE JOURNEY

Have you ever been left out and felt like you didn't belong? How did it feel?

Wherever Jesus went, crowds gathered and pressed in from all sides to hear what He had to say. Word about Jesus kept spreading and began making the religious leaders nervous. On several occasions Jesus freely spoke out against their traditions and religious rules. He was winning the hearts of the people, and for the religious leaders, that was not good.

One day Jesus decided to get away from the crowds and the angry religious leaders. He left Capernaum and went with His disciples into the region of Phoenicia. It was a land of Gentiles (non-Jewish people). Jews never associated with Gentiles, so no one would consider looking for them there. This would be the perfect place to briefly rest and give His disciples some important instruction. Not wanting anyone to know where they were, they entered a house. But they couldn't keep their presence a secret; it wasn't long before someone was standing outside, knocking on the door.

"Oh Jesus," the woman begged, "my daughter has an evil spirit. Could you please drive the demon out of her?"

Jesus looked at the woman. She was a Gentile. Jesus' message and preaching was for the Jews first. But Jesus also knew the Jews would reject His message. In addition, He also knew His message was for all people, regardless of who or what they were. Looking at the woman kindly, Jesus gently tested her faith with a statement.

"Let the children eat all they want," He told her, "for it is not right to take the children's bread and toss it to the dogs."

The region of Phoenicia is today's country of Lebanon.

Usually the word *dog* was a mean word for a Gentile, but Jesus used it differently. He was referring to puppies kept in homes as pets. The woman understood Jesus' meaning. She did not wish to take away His time from teaching His disciples. She did not consider herself as deserving of His attention as a Jewish person might be—after all, she was a Gentile.

"Yes, Lord," she replied, "but even so, the dogs under the table get to eat the children's crumbs."

In those days it was not the custom to eat with forks, knives, and napkins. Instead, people would eat with their hands. When hands became soiled, they would be wiped on a chunk of bread. The bread was then given to the house dogs to eat. This is what the woman was talking about. She was asking only for a portion or scrap of Jesus' favor. She was not asking for a place of honor at the table.

As a result of her humble and faith-filled response, Jesus granted her request. He could have turned her away but didn't. He made Himself available to her and her needs. "For such a reply," Jesus said, "you may go. The demon has left your daughter."

The woman left and returned to her own home. There, she found her daughter resting peacefully and the demon completely gone.

Read Mark 7:24 in your own Bible. What did Jesus desire? What happened? Skip down to verses 29 and 30. Notice what Jesus said and did. Jesus did not show partiality to some and not others; He makes Himself available to everyone. There is no such thing as an unimportant person in Jesus' eyes.

CROSS ROADS

If you were living by Jesus' example and someone outside your group knocked on your door for help, would you help them or would you ignore them?

WHAT'S PRAYER GOT TO DO WITH IT?

TAKEN FROM MARK 9

GETTING READY

Spend some time preparing your heart. Ask God to search your heart and show you what He wants you to learn.

THE JOURNEY

Have you ever been able to do something perfectly well in the past, but suddenly couldn't do it when it counted the most? This kind of failure is what the disciples were experiencing.

"I just don't understand it," one of the disciples said to the other.

"Yes, didn't Jesus give us power and authority to cast out demons?" whispered the other under his breath. The nine disciples stood embarrassed and defeated. The religious leaders who had come to keep track of Jesus were now arguing with the disciples.

"Perhaps Jesus doesn't really have that kind power to give," they challenged. "Perhaps He isn't who He says He is." The crowd standing around didn't know what to think. Loud arguments could be heard between the religious leaders and the disciples.

Suddenly Jesus, Peter, James, and John came walking toward the scene. Thinking Jesus was off traveling somewhere, the religious leaders were amazed to see Him. The crowd ran to greet Jesus.

"What were you arguing about?" Jesus asked the nine disciples.

Before they could answer, a man from the back of the crowd pushed his way forward. "Teacher," he said in despair," I brought my son who is possessed by an evil spirit. Whenever it seizes him, it throws him to the ground. He foams at the mouth, gnashes his teeth, and his body becomes stiff. I asked Your disciples to drive out the spirit, but they could not."

Jesus glanced at His disciples who lowered their heads in defeat. These were the very men Jesus was trying to teach and train. These were the very men who would carry on after He would leave. Did they still not understand?

"Oh unbelieving generation," Jesus sighed, "how long shall I stay with you? How long shall I put up with you? Bring the boy to Me."

The disciples had nothing to say. They just watched as the man brought his son to Jesus. "How long has he been like this?" Jesus asked the father.

"From childhood," he answered. "The demon has often thrown my son into fire or water to kill him. If it is possible that you are able to do anything for him, take pity on us and please help us," he said.

Jesus looked into the man's eyes. He could see the man's faith had been weakened because the disciples couldn't do what they had promised. "If I can?" Jesus asked. "Everything is possible for him who believes," Jesus said, half to the man and half to His disciples.

With these words, the boy's father started to regain his faith. "I do believe," he said, "please help me with my unbelief!"

Noticing a large crowd running to see what was going on, Jesus rebuked the evil spirit. "I command you, come out of him and never enter him again!" Jesus demanded.

The spirit shrieked, shook the boy violently, and came out of him. The boy lay on the ground, looking lifeless. "He's dead!" someone observed. But Jesus took him by the hand and lifted him to his feet. The boy stood up, completely well.

After Jesus left, His disciples asked Him privately, "Why couldn't we drive this demon out? We've driven demons out before with no problem!"

Jesus gently answered, "This kind can come out only by prayer." The disciples grew silent. Jesus had made His point.

CLIMBING ONWARD

Read Mark 9:29 in your own Bible. What was Jesus' answer to the disciples? Do you think they forgot to do something?

DANGER AHEAD

God gives talents and abilities for a reason. Whenever you take them for granted or believe they are from yourself, you will be on dangerous ground and set for failure. There will be times in your life when you'll be tempted to handle things on your own without God. Don't.

GETTING YOUR BEARINGS:
THE BOOK OF LUKE

The book of Luke was written with the Greek person in mind. The Greeks were well–educated and loved arts, beauty, and talking about the meaning of life. They strove to be "perfect" and admired anything or anyone who even came close. In order to be impressed with Jesus, they would need to see Him as the "perfect" man—exactly how Luke portrays Jesus. Being Greek himself, Luke allows us to see the beauty of Jesus' love in becoming a man to save sinners.

As you journey through Luke, notice different things about Jesus. Notice how He willingly limited Himself as a man. See Him praying and weeping. See how He reached out to those whom others hated. Take note of His tenderness and care, yet the power belongs to Him. Allow yourself to walk along beside Him and see the beauty of His love. The Gospel of Luke is packed with great stuff; enjoy your journey!

AND STAY OUT!

TAKEN FROM LUKE 8

GETTING READY

Take a few moments to pray. Simply ask God to challenge you today, and give Him permission to speak to your heart. Thank Him that He has power over evil.

THE JOURNEY

How do you feel when you see something evil?

Jesus' foot stepped out of the boat and onto the sandy shore. He and His disciples had just crossed the Sea of Galilee and were now in a different region. Suddenly, a loud voice shrieked out, "What do You want to do with me, Jesus, Son of the Most High God? I beg You, don't torture me!"

The voice came from a man who was naked and dirty, with broken chains dangling from his arms and legs. He had a wild and almost savage look in his eyes, and by the looks of the broken chains, he also had super-human strength. The townspeople had chained up this demon-possessed man, but he had broken the chains as if they were only string. Instead of living in a house, the man lived among the tombs in the graveyard. Now he was on his knees before Jesus—not in worship, but to beg for mercy.

"Son of the Most High God" were the words the demon spoke through the man. These were not words of respect, but general words used to describe deity without giving worship and respect.

Jesus looked into the wild eyes of the man. "What is your name?"

The demons spoke through the man. "Legion," they answered, "for there are many of us." The people who heard this backed up in fear. "Legion" was a word used to describe an army of about one thousand soldiers! No wonder this man is beast-like, they thought, he has an army of demons living in him!

Jesus was not afraid; He had power over the demons and they knew it. They only wanted to destroy the man's life. At the sight of Jesus, the demons became terrified; they knew Jesus was the giver of life.

The demons begged Jesus not to order them into the Abyss (their place of eternal punishment). They knew it is where they were sentenced to go, but were uncertain of the timing. They pleaded with Jesus and begged for mercy. Seeing a large herd of pigs on a nearby hillside, the demons begged Jesus again. "Please, allow us to enter into those pigs," they pleaded.

Jesus looked at the pigs. It was not God's timing to send the demons into the Abyss, so He gave the demons permission to enter the pigs.

With a loud scream, the demons left the man and entered into the pigs on the hillside. As a result, the pigs went instantly wild. They ran around confused, then rushed down the steep bank into the lake and drowned. The farmers tending the pigs saw this strange behavior, and ran off to tell the people in the countryside and town.

People began coming to see this strange happening for themselves. As they approached Jesus, they saw the once naked and demon-possessed man dressed and in his right mind. They were afraid.

"Jesus cured this demon-possessed man!" came the report from those who had seen it. Many of the townspeople were thinking of the loss of the herd of pigs. "If this is what Jesus does, maybe He'd better leave before we have anymore losses," they reasoned. They were more concerned about making money and living a comfortable life than they were

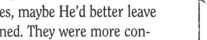

about the man Jesus healed. Being selfishly afraid, they wanted no part with Jesus and asked Him to leave their land. Jesus did.

While climbing into the boat, the man who was set free from the demons asked Jesus if he could come along. Jesus tenderly responded, "I need you to stay here and tell these people how much God has done for you." The man agreed and went away, unafraid to tell the whole town what Jesus had personally done for him.

CLIMBING ONWARD

In your own Bible, read Luke 8:31-32. What does it say? What were the demons doing? Who seems in control here?

Skill Time

Demons are very real. They are Satan's army whose job is to do everything in their power to destroy people and keep them from knowing God. They are powerful, but do not have absolute power. Their end is final, certain, and soon coming—a fact they know very well.

What do you fear? Right now, spend a few minutes telling Jesus about some scary thoughts you keep having or a fear you have been struggling with. Thank Jesus for His power over evil, and ask Him to protect you and calm your heart. He will.

OH, I KNOW!

GETTING READY

Take a few minutes to quiet your thoughts. Ask God to search your heart, and teach you what He wants you to learn.

THE JOURNEY

Did you ever give the right answer to a question your teacher asked but didn't understand what your answer really meant?

Jesus' face was set toward Jerusalem as He prayed. He knew it wouldn't be long before He would go there to die on a cross. Jesus looked over at them; time was running out. He must find out where they stood, then train and lead them onward from there. Turning to His disciples, Jesus asked, "Who do the crowds say that I am?" He started with a question that would be easy for them to answer.

"Some say John the Baptist," replied one disciple.

"Others say Elijah," answered another.

The rest of the disciples said, "We have heard people say You must be one of the prophets come back to life."

Jesus looked directly into their eyes and challenged them. It was time for them to understand for themselves. "But who do *you* say that I am?" Jesus challenged.

Silence fell over the disciples. Some of them were not quite sure what they thought. They had seen Jesus do many wonderful miracles of healing the blind, casting out demons, stilling storms, and teaching with authority. They knew Jesus was not a mere man, and yet . . .

A voice suddenly broke the silence. "You are the Christ of God–the Messiah!" Peter answered. All the other disciples turned to look at Peter. His eyes shone with delight as he thought about how the Messiah would squash all the Jews' enemies. From childhood he had been taught about the coming Messiah. Now, living under the rule of the Romans, Peter thought it was the perfect time for the Messiah to come. *At last we Jews will be free!* he thought to himself.

Jesus knew Peter's thoughts. Peter had the right answer but didn't quite understand what that answer really meant. Jesus strictly warned Peter and the disciples not to tell anyone. First He would have to teach them God's plan for the Messiah.

The Jews believed a great prophet would come before the Messiah, and some mistakenly thought Jesus was that prophet. They expected the Messiah to be a political king who would lead them into great victories as a nation.

"I must suffer many things and be rejected by the chief priests and teachers of the law," Jesus told them. "After that, I will be killed, but I will raise back to life on the third day."

Peter stood amazed. The words confused all of them. Peter gave the right answer, and yet there were so many things he didn't understand about the answer he gave. Peter decided in his heart to know this Jesus better.

CLIMBING ONWARD

Using your own Bible, look up Luke 9:20 and read it aloud. Now, read it again, substituting your name for *you* and the verb *does* for *do*. Was this a group question or a personal one? What did Jesus ask?

THINKING on your FEET

If Jesus were to ask you the question in verse 20, how would you answer? Do you really understand the answer you would give?

HEY, IT'S A PARTY!

TAKEN FROM LUKE 9

GETTING READY

Stop and pray. Ask God to help you see anew the greatness and glory surrounding Jesus.

THE JOURNEY

Did you ever get so excited about a great idea you had, that you spoke without really thinking first? What did you say?

Peter rubbed his eyes and looked up. Could this be a dream? Only moments ago he and a few others had come up the mountain with Jesus to pray. Perhaps they had dozed off for a few minutes, but they weren't sleeping now. They were fully awake and amazed at the strange and wonderful thing that was happening before their very eyes!

While Jesus was praying, His face began to look different. His clothes became unusually white and started to gleam. The gleaming clothes almost hurt Peter's eyes, much like looking directly into the sun. The brightness was like lightning. Jesus was not alone, but stood talking with two men who had appeared. Peter strained and shielded his eyes to see better. Could it be? One man was Moses and the other Elijah!

Long ago, God had given the Ten Commandments to Moses. Elijah was a great prophet whom God had used. Many Jews believe Elijah to be connected with the end times and the coming of the Messiah. Moses reminded the Jews of the past; Elijah reminded them of the future. Both men left the world in a strange way. Moses was buried by the Lord (Deuteronomy 34: 5, 6), and Elijah was taken to heaven in a whirlwind (II Kings 2:11). Now they both stood together, talking with Jesus.

Peter couldn't believe his eyes. Here, talking with Jesus were the two greatest Jewish heroes that had ever lived! Wondering what they were talking about, Peter scooted closer to listen. He sat breathless as he heard Jesus talking with Moses and Elijah. Jesus spoke about the things He was going to accomplish in Jerusalem, and they seemed to be discussing Jesus' departure from earth. It almost seemed as if Jesus were the fulfillment of all that Moses and Elijah had spoken.

> This event has been commonly called the Transfiguration. To be transfigured means to change in appearance. This could also be called a metamorphosis, a word used to describe the changing of a caterpillar into a butterfly.

Peter gasped in wonder and delight. As a child he had learned about Moses and Elijah. Now they stood before him! He could hardly contain himself.

"Master, it is good for us to be here!" Peter exclaimed. The words exploded excitedly from his mouth as he came up with an idea. "I know, let's make three huts of shelter so we can all stay here. One for You, one for Moses, and one for Elijah!"

Peter didn't know what he was saying. A huge cloud surrounded them, and Peter and the other two disciples became afraid. A loud voice from heaven exploded, "This is My Son. My Chosen One, listen to Him."

When the cloud lifted, the disciples were left standing face to face with Jesus. Moses and Elijah had gone.

Peter didn't know that his idea of three shelters suggested Jesus was only equal to Moses and Elijah—when in fact, Jesus was much greater!

However, God had just made that point very clear! Peter didn't realize that by suggesting they build three shelters, he was suggesting Jesus needn't go anywhere—even to Jerusalem to die on the cross! Peter had spoken out of turn, and now that the disciples were left face to face with Jesus, Peter began to realize his mistake. Only six to eight days ago Peter had declared Jesus to be the Messiah; today it seemed he had forgotten. Peter and the disciples were quiet. They would treasure in their hearts the wonderful thing they had just seen and experienced.

CLIMBING ONWARD

Turn in your Bible to Luke 9:35 and read it. What does it say? What three specific things did God say about Jesus? What do they mean?

CROSS ROADS

When you get excited about opportunities in front of you, whose plans will you consider first: God's or your own?

LOOK WHAT I DID!

TAKEN FROM LUKE 10

GETTING READY

Before you journey into God's Word today, ask Him to speak to your heart. Give Him permission to point out the things He wants you to learn or change.

THE JOURNEY

How do you feel when other kids brag about what they can do–secretly comparing themselves to others and assuming they are better? That's a danger Jesus addressed.

Jesus had a busy schedule and knew His time on earth was running out. Jesus sent about seventy men to tell others of God's coming kingdom. The groups went out in pairs. All were given specific instructions.

Jesus told them, "I am sending you out as lambs in the midst of wolves." He warned them of possible danger and their own helplessness. He didn't want them to be distracted by belongings. He said, "Don't carry a bag full of belongings or extra shoes. And when you see someone on the road, do not stop to greet them." Greeting customs of the time were very long and involved and could distract the disciples from the importance of their task. The disciples were to stay at the first home they came to. If a city would not receive their message, they were to shake the dust off their feet—a customary warning of being rejected. Those people would not be part of God's Kingdom.

The seventy had done exactly as Jesus instructed, and now they were returning with wonderful reports. "Jesus!" one of the disciples reported, "We were able to do amazing things!"

Traveling prophets (both good and bad) became so common that rules were made concerning them. One rule stated that a prophet staying in a house longer than three days without working was to be considered a false prophet.

"Yes," said another breathlessly, "we even had power over demons—in Your name, of course!" Their faces were radiant with confidence.

Jesus looked into their faces and could see they were caught up in their own excitement and successes. Perhaps some were even comparing their adventures and accomplishments to others who had gone out. They would be tempted to measure what they had done, then become prideful and think they were better than others.

Jesus replied, "I was watching Satan fall from heaven like lightning." Jesus recalled how Satan was once an important angel in heaven. Because of his pride and wanting to take God's throne for himself, Satan was cast out of heaven.

"I gave you power and authority over serpents and scorpions, and over all the power of the enemy," Jesus told them. "Yet, do not rejoice in this and the things you were able to accomplish," Jesus challenged. "Rather, rejoice that your names are recorded in heaven."

Jesus didn't want them to get sidetracked by all the things they could do, but rather to remember they were working for God. They needed to keep their hearts focused on Him and the things that would really last. They needed to recall the things God did in and through them, rather than what they did in their own efforts.

CLIMBING ONWARD

In your Bible, look up Luke 10:20. What do the last nine or ten words of that verse say?

CROSS ROADS

Do you base your feelings about yourself (good or bad) on what others say or do, or on the fact that you know and are known by Jesus?

LET ME THINK ABOUT IT . . .

TAKEN FROM LUKE 14

GETTING READY

Find a quiet place where you can be alone. Pray, asking God to speak to your heart. Ask Him to help you understand the importance of being committed wholeheartedly to Jesus.

THE JOURNEY

Do you know friends who are quick to go along with something but soon drop out when they see it might cost them time or effort?

People came from near and far just to see and hear Jesus. Some decided to follow Jesus no matter what. Others were tagging along halfheartedly. To the second group, Jesus turned and gave an eye-opening challenge.

Jesus spoke saying, "If anyone comes to Me and does not love Me more than his parents, brothers, sisters, the one he is married to, and even his own life . . . he cannot be My disciple."

To get His point across, Jesus used the word *hate*. A person's love for others should look almost like hate when compared with his love for Jesus. This statement wiped a few smiles off the faces of some in the crowd. They loved others more than they loved Him.

Jesus continued on, "Anyone who does not carry his cross and follow me cannot be my disciple."

It was not uncommon to see a man carrying a cross through the heart of the city. When the Roman Empire punished a criminal with crucifixion, the criminal was forced to carry his own cross part of the way. Cross carrying declared to all bystanders that the Roman Empire was right, and its ways just. Jesus applied this example to discipleship. Jesus' ways are right, and those who would follow Him must have their eyes set on a one–way road. They must carry their cross and follow Him always.

> **Discipleship is the act of allowing Jesus to be Lord over your life. It is giving Him everything you are or ever will be, and making a commitment to follow Him with your whole heart.**

When Jesus said this, a few in the crowd grew uncomfortable. They weren't sure they were willing to do that. They had things to do, places to go, and people to see! Perhaps after they had lived a life of pleasure they would return and follow Jesus.

Some in the crowd looked at Jesus with eager eyes. They were willing to do anything, and why not? It all sounded like such an adventure! To these people Jesus gave another illustration.

"Suppose one of you wants to build a tower," Jesus said. "You would sit down and plan the cost before beginning to build. Otherwise, if you started the tower and weren't able to finish it, you would be laughed at."

The people understood what Jesus was saying. Towers were commonly built in vineyards where a man could keep watch to make sure thieves didn't steal the harvest. A half-built tower was not only laughed at, it was useless.

Jesus continued, "So it is with discipleship. A person must count the cost and commitment before he follows Me."

The crowd grew restless. Some who were on the edge slipped away, unnoticed. They knew their hearts were not right. Others listened closely; they had never heard such words. Being a follower of Jesus was not something one did because others were doing it. It was not something you took lightly, nor did halfheartedly. There was a personal cost and commitment involved. Being a follower of Jesus might mean giving up earthly things, *but* the blessings gained far outweigh them!

In your Bible, look up Luke 14:27. (Go on, look it up!) Read it aloud a few times and think about it. Jesus expects commitment from us. Sometimes the road may be hard, but Jesus has traveled it before us. He's already been there and knows what He is asking us to do.

Skill Time

Tell Jesus what is going through your mind right now. Don't be afraid; He already knows what you are thinking. Be honest and explain to Him all the reasons in your life why it is difficult for you to follow Him. Ask Him to change your heart and desires and to make you a true disciple of His.

HE'S YOUR FRIEND?

TAKEN FROM LUKE 19

GETTING READY

Spend a few moments in prayer. Be honest and real before God. Ask Him to forgive you for any wrong attitudes or actions in your life.

THE JOURNEY

Ever notice how some kids strive to be included with the popular or cool group at school? They fear what others might think of them, so they try to make themselves look good by who their friends are. Jesus did the opposite.

"Hey, I heard Jesus is passing through Jericho!" shouted one person to another. Soon a small group of people had gathered along the road where Jesus would soon pass. People stretched their necks and stood on tiptoe trying to see Jesus. Those who arrived late tried to catch a glimpse of Jesus. Zacchaeus was one of those people.

Zacchaeus was not a well-liked man; he was hated by almost everyone. Zacchaeus was a chief tax collector and worked for the Roman Empire—enemies of the Jews. A tax collector gathered a certain amount of money from every household. This money was turned over to the Roman Empire. Any extra money the tax collector collected (above what was required), he was allowed to keep for himself.

Zacchaeus charged especially high rates, keeping more money for himself. Because he worked for the Romans, people had to pay him. They gave their money out of fear of punishment. This made them hate Zacchaeus even more.

Zacchaeus heard that Jesus was a friend of tax collectors. Oh, how he needed such a friend! The whole town hated Zacchaeus, and his heart ached with loneliness. Yet money held too tight a grip for him to give up his job. Zacchaeus knew that going out into the crowd could be dangerous.

As Zacchaeus approached the back of the crowd, a strange thing happened. The crowd bunched together in order to keep Zacchaeus out. Hot anger rose in his cheeks as he heard the snickers from the townspeople. *So, this is their game*, he may have thought. Not wanting to miss the only One who might accept him, Zacchaeus ran ahead. There, he climbed a tree with a low trunk and spread-out branches, hoping to see Jesus as He walked past. Zacchaeus was not ready for what happened next.

> Jericho, the City of Palms, was an important and wealthy town located in the Jordan Valley. Jericho had a great palm forest and balsam groves that gave off fragrances for miles around. Its dates and balsam were carried by the Romans to worldwide trade routes.

Passing under the tree, Jesus stopped and looked up. "Zacchaeus," He said, "come down from that tree, for I must stay at your house today."

Zacchaeus nearly fell down in all his excitement!

The crowd who saw this began to murmur. "Jesus is going to be the guest of a *sinner*!" they gasped with disapproval. They could not believe Jesus would choose to be seen with a person like Zacchaeus!

Zacchaeus was overcome with joy. He saw the love and acceptance in Jesus' eyes and immediately became a changed man. He would serve and love Jesus with his whole heart from here on out. Having become a new person, Zacchaeus then proved it with his actions.

"Look, Lord," Zacchaeus said, "I now give half of my possessions to the poor. For those I have cheated, I will pay back four times the amount." This was more than the law required for thieves to repay!

Jesus smiled at Zacchaeus. "Today, salvation has come to this house." Zacchaeus's life had changed, and all because Jesus sought him out. "The Son of Man came to seek and to save what was lost," Jesus said.

CLIMBING ONWARD

Look up Luke 19:7 in your own Bible and read it for yourself. Then skip down and read verse 10. What do you think is most important to Jesus? Do you think there is ever anyone too sinful for Him to forgive and love?

CROSS ROADS

How will you respond with the message of God's love? Will you choose to stand back with your friends and look cool, or will you talk to someone that no one else will talk to?

GETTING YOUR BEARINGS:

THE BOOK OF JOHN

Each Gospel gives us yet another view of Jesus. As we put them all together, we can paint a better picture of who Jesus is. Let's take a minute and quickly review what we have learned so far. Matthew shows Jesus as a King fulfilling prophecies. Mark shows Jesus as a servant and describes many of His miracles. Luke lets us see Jesus as the perfect man, and we see the beauty of His love. The last sketch in our portrait of Jesus is the book of John. John opens our eyes to understand and see Jesus as He is and always will be . . . God.

Our journey through John will begin with the first miracle Jesus did and continue onward. As you journey through John, notice the lives Jesus touched and how He touched them. See by what authority He did these things, and listen to the claims He made about Himself.

WHO'D HAVE THOUGHT IT!

TAKEN FROM JOHN 2

GETTING READY

Prepare your heart for today's journey into God's Word by spending a few minutes in prayer. Ask God to show you special things from His Word today.

THE JOURNEY

Have you ever been asked to do something that didn't make sense to you and felt like it was a waste of your time?

"Do what?" the servants asked. The wedding celebration had run out of wine. It was an insult to the guests for a host not to have enough to eat and drink. Something must be done, but what?

Because Mary was helping with the wedding celebration, she told the servants to find Jesus. Mary knew if anyone could help, Jesus could. She instructed the servants to do whatever Jesus said.

"Fill these pots with water," Jesus instructed as he pointed to six stone jars. Each held almost thirty gallons of water—the size of a bathtub! It would take quite a while to fill all of them.

"What does this have to do with being out of wine?" they spoke privately to each other as they worked at filling the pots.

"I don't know. Perhaps Jesus didn't understand what we were telling Him," the other replied. It was a slow job. Little by little the water levels rose in the stone pots. Finally, they were completely full. The servants reported back to Jesus for His next instructions. *Perhaps now He will tell us where we can get some wine*, they thought.

These stone jars were not meant to be drunk from but were to be used for special washing ceremonies.

"Go to the pots you just filled with water," Jesus told them. "Draw some out with the dipper and take it to the head waiter."

The servants were shocked. By doing such a thing they could be fired! Yet they recalled Mary's words and obeyed Jesus. They did exactly as Jesus said.

The servants looked at the dipper as it went into the cool water and came up full. It was clear and didn't look like wine. With trembling hand, they brought the dipper of water to the head-waiter. They closed their eyes, expecting the worst as he lifted the dipper to his lips.

"Where did this come from?" the headwaiter demanded. It's the best wine yet!"

The servants were amazed! Only moments ago it had been water; how could this be? The servants looked at Jesus with both awe and wonder.

This was just the beginning of the miracles Jesus did that showed His power and glory.

CLIMBING ONWARD

Turn to John 2:5 in your Bible. What does it say? One of the interesting things about Jesus' first miracle was not what He did, but that He chose to use people to do it. Jesus used people who were simply willing to do as He asked.

Skill Time

God does not need people who are able to do things well. He needs people who are willing to do as He asks. He will take care of the rest.

If you desire to be like the servants and be used by God, take a moment right now and tell Him that.

It's No Secret ... Anymore

TAKEN FROM JOHN 3

Getting Ready

Take some time to talk with God. Ask Him to speak to your heart and help you to see how He can change lives from the inside out.

The Journey

What do you think when someone you know begins to change and do unexpected things?

"Rabbi, we know you're a teacher from God. No one could do the miraculous signs you are doing if God were not with him," the man said. He was a Pharisee and member of the Sanhedrin.

Many members of the Sanhedrin considered Jesus an uneducated and self-made rabbi. "Jesus didn't go through the years of schooling I went through!" they muttered under their breath. "Yet so many people follow Him and listen to His teachings!" others said in a jealous tone of voice. The religious leaders had a growing dislike of Jesus and watched Him carefully.

Nicodemus and Joseph of Arimathea, also members of the

Sanhedrin, had an interest in Jesus but for different reasons. They too had heard reports about the teachings of Jesus and the wonderful miracles He had performed. No self-made rabbi could do these things, they thought, *Jesus must be a teacher from God*!

Nicodemus needed to find out for himself. He slipped out in the dark of night to see Jesus. A night visit would allow secrecy and give Nicodemus an opportunity to catch Jesus alone and away from the crowds. Nicodemus looked over his shoulder. Seeing Jesus could be risky and might cause trouble if the other Pharisees found out.

> **The Sanhedrin was made up of seventy religious leaders and acted like a Supreme Court for the Jews.**

"I tell you the truth," Jesus said to Nicodemus, "no one can see the kingdom of God unless he is born again."

Those words hit Nicodemus like a bomb. He was from a good family, held a high and important religious position, and was wealthy. Why wouldn't he see the kingdom of God? The words Jesus spoke seemed strange. "Be born again?" Nicodemus asked, "I've already been born, and now I am old! I can't go back into my mother's womb—no one can!"

"You are Israel's teacher," Jesus replied gently, "and yet you do not understand this?" Jesus continued on, explaining to Nicodemus what being born-again meant. Then He explained how the Son of Man must die on a cross in order to save people from the wickedness of their sins.

Jesus told Nicodemus about God's tender love and compassion. "For God so loved the world that He provided His one and only Son, that whoever believes in Him shall not perish but have eternal life."

Nicodemus looked thoughtful. He wanted what Jesus talked about but needed time to think.

CLIMBING ONWARD

We don't know exactly what Nicodemus decided, but we do see him mysteriously changing. Look up John 3:2. What does this tell you? Now read John 7:50, 51. What was Nicodemus doing here? Notice a difference in him? Fearful Nicodemus had courage to speak up for Jesus. Lastly, turn to John 19:39, 40. What is Nicodemus publicly doing? Notice how much he brought! He would almost need a wheelbarrow to carry it through town—it would be hard to be secretive about that!

CROSS ROADS

By your actions, can others tell you love Jesus, or are you still working secretly—in the dark?

I PLEDGE ALLEGIANCE

TAKEN FROM JOHN 9

GETTING READY

Get alone with God for a few minutes. Tell Him about the things that matter to you. Ask Him to search your heart and help you to be the person He wants you to be.

THE JOURNEY

Are you willing to stand for something you know is true, even when you're the only one standing for it?

As Jesus and the disciples were leaving the Temple they saw a man who had been blind since birth. "Teacher," the disciples asked curiously, "who sinned—this man or his parents—that he was born blind?"

"Neither," Jesus replied, "his blindness is so that God's work can be displayed in his life."

With that, Jesus bent down, spat on the ground to make mud, and gently placed some on the man's eyes. "Go wash in the Pool of Siloam," Jesus instructed.

The man left to do exactly as Jesus said.

As cool water dripped down the man's face, he began to see something! "What was that?" he breathed excitedly. Slowly the black shadows began to melt into shapes and color. *Could that be a bird?* he asked himself with delight. "And those must be flowers!" he exclaimed with great joy. "Hey! I can see! I can see!"

Quickly he ran back. Those at the temple couldn't believe it was him. "It can't be," they whispered to one another. "This man must be someone who just looks like the blind beggar!"

The healed man insisted he was the blind beggar, and the people looked at him suspiciously. "Tell us how your eyes were opened!" they demanded.

The beggar told them exactly what Jesus had done.

"The man who healed you is not from God," they protested. "A man of God would not heal on the Sabbath. Where is this man?"

"I don't know," answered the healed man.

Unable to find Jesus to ask him questions, the people took the man to the Pharisees who were not so excited. Not too long ago, Jesus had healed a person on the Sabbath day and then made claims to be God! Because of that, the religious leaders made a law warning that if anyone even said Jesus was the Christ, they would be kicked out of the synagogue forever.

The Pharisees weren't convinced of what the blind man said so they sent for his parents to identify him.

"Yes, this is our son," they said. When asked why their son was able to see, the parents said, Jesus had miraculously healed their son, but if they said so, they could be thrown out of the synagogue! "Why don't you ask him? He is old enough to speak for himself!"

So the Pharisees summoned the healed man again. "Give glory to God. Jesus is a sinner since He healed on the Sabbath. He is not from God," they flatly stated.

The blind man looked at them. It was wonderful to see the things he had only heard or imagined before. This was truly a miracle. "Whether He is a sinner or not, I don't know. But one thing I do know—once I was blind, but now I see!"

The Pharisees didn't like that answer. "What did Jesus do to you?" they demanded. "How did He open your eyes?"

"I told you already and you didn't listen," the man replied. "Why do you want to hear it again? Do you want to become His disciples too?" the blind man challenged.

The Pharisees grew angry. "You are a follower of Jesus! We are followers of Moses! We know that God spoke to Moses, but as for this Jesus who healed you, we don't even know where He comes from!" they shouted.

"I find that amazing," the healed man answered. "You don't know where He comes from, yet He opened my eyes. We know that God doesn't listen to sinners, but only to a godly man who does His will. Opening the eyes of a man born blind is no small thing. This man couldn't have done what He did unless He was from God."

It was often and mistakenly thought that someone's ill fortune (being blind, crippled, etc.) came as a result of that person's sin. Not so!

The religious leaders began to cast insults at the healed man. They attacked him with words, "You were born blind because you were unworthy. How dare you talk to us in such a way!" With that they threw him out of the synagogue and forbade him to come back.

When Jesus heard about this, He came looking for the man. "Do you believe in God's special Son?" Jesus asked.

"Yes, I do, but who is He?" the man replied.

Jesus tenderly answered, "You are seeing Him now; He is the one speaking with you now."

"Lord, I believe," the man said, overwhelmed with joy. He fell to his knees in worship.

CLIMBING ONWARD

Look up John 9:25 in your own Bible. How did the man respond to the angry accusations of the religious leaders? Look at the words carefully. The man had experienced something for himself, and no one could deny or take that from him.

DANGER AHEAD

If you make a stand for Jesus, you may face being called names, being threatened by others, or being pushed out of your group of friends.

As Jesus came looking for the man who honored Him, He will come looking for you and stand by your side. Don't be afraid to stand on the things you know for sure. Jesus stands there with you.

I KNOW THAT VOICE!

TAKEN FROM JOHN 10

GETTING READY

As you prepare for your journey through God's Word, ask Jesus to help you trust in His caring nature.

THE JOURNEY

How would it make you feel to know someone cares for you no matter what you do, is always there for you, and will fight to protect you?

"I am the Good Shepherd," Jesus said. "The Good Shepherd lays down His life for the sheep." His words were simple yet packed with meaning. The crowd listened contentedly; sheep and shepherds were things they were familiar with, yet somehow Jesus added new meaning.

Everyone knew the lives of sheep depended heavily upon their shepherd. In the evening, wild animals, such as lions, bears, and wolves, were a constant danger. It was not uncommon for shepherds concerned only for their own wages to run in fear and leave the flock of sheep behind. They didn't care because the sheep were not their own.

Jesus told how He was the Good Shepherd; He would lay down His life to protect and defend even the littlest of sheep.

Part of a shepherd's job was to continually move his sheep to greener pastures to graze. If he didn't, the sheep would graze too much in one spot and ruin the land. Ruined land meant disease and no food for the sheep.

Sometimes the shepherd would sense his sheep getting frightened and would walk among them—perhaps making clicking sounds to let them know of his presence. This helped to comfort and calm the sheep.

Shepherds protect and sometimes rescue sheep. A simple drink from a fast–moving stream could result in disaster for the sheep. Some might get carried downstream and others drown because their wool soaked up water and weighed them down. When it was necessary for sheep to cross a stream, they knew the safest spot was right next to the shepherd; he would protect them.

A good shepherd knew his sheep and gave each one a name. In the morning hours, the shepherd would go to a walled sheep pen where other sheep were kept. Each shepherd called his flock out from among the others and led them to pasture. The sheep knew their shepherd's voice and would willingly come. If a stranger called them, they would not respond because they didn't recognize the voice.

At night the shepherd would find an area that was closed in on three sides by rocks or other barriers. He would then lie down and close off the fourth side with his own body. He became the door or gate to the pen.

"I am the gate," Jesus said to His listeners. "Whoever enters through Me will be saved. A thief comes only to kill, steal, and destroy. I have come to bring life."

Jesus' words rang true as the crowd realized they were like the sheep in need of a shepherd—not just any shepherd, but Jesus the Good Shepherd. They understood how Jesus would watch after those who followed Him, and always be there to lead those who are His own. Jesus the Good Shepherd not only cares for His sheep, but also backs up His words with His very life.

CLIMBING ONWARD

In your own Bible, turn to John 10:14 and read it. In what ways does this verse describe you?

DANGER AHEAD

Just as Jesus talked about thieves and robbers, there will be false shepherds who will try to get you to follow them. They may promise you special privileges or abilities. They may promise you greener pastures. Don't be fooled; know and follow Jesus' voice only. He has proven His worthiness. He is the Shepherd who lays down His life for you.

Now, This Is Serious Stuff

TAKEN FROM JOHN 11—12

Getting Ready

Stop and pray. Ask God to give you wisdom to understand His Word, and an open heart to examine your own life.

THE Journey

Have you ever desired for your life to be important; to really count for something?

"But Lord," the disciples pleaded, "you can't go back to Judea! Remember the Jews tried to stone you there?" The disciples couldn't believe what Jesus wanted to do.

It had been two days since Jesus got word that His dear friend Lazarus was sick. Jesus dearly loved Lazarus and his sisters, Martha and Mary. Yet Jesus purposefully waited before going to see them, knowing certain things must first happen for God to be glorified.

"Lazarus has died," Jesus told His disciples plainly. "For your sake I'm glad I wasn't there, so that you might see what I am about to do, and believe. Let's go to Judea."

Thomas couldn't believe what was happening; he was sure Jesus would be killed. He said to the disciples, "Let's go, so we may all die together."

As Jesus approached the village of Bethany, Martha ran to meet him. "Lord, if you had been here, my brother would have lived," she said, out of breath. "I know nothing is impossible with You and that God will give You whatever you ask."

Jesus lovingly responded, "Your brother will rise again." Mary knew Lazarus would rise in the great resurrection, but Jesus was talking about right now. "I am the resurrection and the life. He who believes in Me will live, even though his body dies. Whoever lives and believes in Me will live eternally. Do you believe this?" Jesus asked her.

Being a witness and giving a testimony means presenting the facts and evidence of something you know or have experienced personally.

"Yes, Lord," Mary replied, "I believe You are the Christ, God's Son who has come into the world."

With that, Martha ran off to get Mary who was still at home. When Mary heard that Jesus asked for her, she jumped up and ran out the door. The mourners who were with her followed, thinking she went to the tomb to weep.

When Mary reached the place where Jesus was, she fell at His feet. "Lord, if You had been here, my brother wouldn't have died!" she said with grief.

When Jesus saw her weeping and all the others who had come along, He was deeply moved. "Where did you lay him?" Jesus asked tenderly.

"Come, we will show you," they said. Jesus wept because of His love for Lazarus and his sisters.

Those in the crowd said, "See how much Jesus loved him?" Others said, "If He could open the eyes of a blind man why couldn't He have kept Lazarus from dying?" They did not know God's plan.

Arriving at the tomb, Jesus ordered the stone rolled away. "But he has been dead for over four days!" they protested. "He will smell!"

"Did I not say you would see the glory of God if you believed?" Jesus asked.

With that, they rolled away the stone. Jesus looked up to heaven and prayed so those around could hear. "Father, I thank You that You have heard Me. I know You always hear Me, but I say this for the benefit of those standing here."

Then Jesus called out loudly, "Lazarus, come out!" Lazarus, once dead, appeared at the entrance of the tomb—fully alive! Jesus instructed the people to remove Lazarus's grave clothes.

When the crowd saw this, they were stunned! Many put their faith in Jesus, but some reported to the Pharisees what Jesus had done.

The Pharisees and chief priests called a meeting of the Sanhedrin. "Look what's happening here! This man is doing many miraculous signs. If we let Him continue, everyone will believe in Him!" From that day on, the religious leaders plotted ways to kill Jesus.

Time passed, and it was now six days before the Passover celebration. Jesus went to a dinner held in His honor at Mary, Martha, and Lazarus's home in Bethany. They wanted to show Jesus how grateful they were.

The raising of Lazarus created quite a stir. Word about the miracle had spread fast! Large crowds stopped by Mary and Martha's home. They came not only to see Jesus, but also Lazarus whom He had brought back to life! When the chief priests heard about this, they wanted to kill Lazarus also, for he too was dangerous to their cause. On account of Lazarus's life, many Jews put their faith in Jesus.

CLIMBING ONWARD

Look up John 12:11 in your Bible. Read it once to yourself, then read it aloud and substitute your name for "him" and the word "people" where it says many of the Jews. Think about what you just read.

Skill Time

Does your life speak of the greatness of God? On a piece of paper, write down a few sentences about what your life was like before you came to know Jesus (fearful, always angry, trouble making, selfish, etc.). Now write a sentence about how God is changing you, or about what He means to you. You have just written down your testimony! Don't worry if you couldn't come up with something spectacular. God often works in small and quiet ways. Pray about one person you can share your testimony with this week and do it. If you're uncertain that you even have a personal relationship with Jesus, turn to the back of this book and prayerfully read the message that's there for you.

Don't Worry about It

TAKEN FROM JOHN 13—16

Getting Ready

As you prepare to journey through God's Word, ask Him to help you learn more about His unconditional love.

The Journey

Have you ever experienced being around someone who knows your weaknesses but loves you regardless of the hurtful things you might say or do? How does it feel to have someone who cares for you deeply and looks out for your best interest?

Jesus looked at His disciples. He knew the strengths and weaknesses of each, yet He loved them beyond measure. Jesus knew the time with His disciples was short. Although there were many things He wanted to tell them, He most wanted to encourage them. Jesus knew the days ahead would be one of the toughest tests they would ever face.

"I'm going to tell you something now before it happens, so when it does, you will believe all the more that I am who I say I am," Jesus said. They listened curiously as He continued. "One of you will betray Me."

The disciples immediately looked at one another. *Who could it be?*

"Who is it, Lord?" John asked.

Jesus answered, "It is the one to whom I give this piece of bread." He handed the bread to Judas, but the other disciples didn't notice. "What you do, do quickly," Jesus told Judas before he slipped away into the night.

Jesus continued, "I am going to be with you for just a little while longer. You will look for Me but won't be able to find Me. Where I am going you cannot come."

"Lord," Simon Peter blurted out, "why can't I follow You now? I'm willing to lay down my life for You!"

Knowing Peter's weaknesses, Jesus patiently answered, "Will you really lay down your life for Me, Peter? . . . Before the rooster crows, you will say you never knew Me—not one time, but three separate times."

Jesus turned to His disciples. "Don't be worried about what will happen. Trust in God and trust also in Me. I'm going to the Father to prepare a place for you in heaven, and just as I go, I will come back. I am the Way, the Truth, and the Life; no one can come to the Father except through Me."

Jesus explained how the Holy Spirit would be sent to comfort them. "My peace I give to you. Don't be troubled or worried," He comforted. Jesus then explained how He was like a vine and they were the branches. They would have all they needed if they stuck to Him.

The disciples listened, but their minds wandered back to what Jesus had said earlier. *What does Jesus mean by 'a little while and you will see Me no more, then after a little while you will see Me'?*

Knowing the disciples didn't understand, Jesus explained it this way, "I came from God the Father and entered the world. Now I am leaving the world and going back to heaven."

"We understand!" they exclaimed, "We believe You came from God!"

"At last you believe!" Jesus answered. He rejoiced that they understood, but He also knew how weak they would be. Jesus knew in His hour of need they would turn their backs and run in fear for their own lives. He could have been disappointed in the disciples or tried to make them feel bad in advance, but He didn't. No matter what their actions, He would always love His disciples and keep their best interest in mind. His telling them in advance what would happen was an act of love and encouragement to prepare them.

Jesus' face was full of love and concern. "I have told you these things so that you may have peace in Me. You are going to have trouble in this world, but don't be discouraged! I have overcome the world."

CLIMBING ONWARD

Read John 16:33 in your own Bible. Jesus tells his disciples three different facts. What does He say?

Skill Time

What worries you? What takes away your peace? Jesus made you special and He is concerned about the things that concern you. Take an index card or a piece of paper and write down three things you are most concerned about. Next, write John 16:33 across the top. Spend a few minutes thanking Jesus that He is bigger than any problem you could ever face. Ask Him to give you His peace and strength to deal with your problems.

YEAH? PROVE IT!

TAKEN FROM JOHN 18

GETTING READY

Pray before you journey through God's Word. Ask God to speak to your heart and help you better appreciate Jesus' determination to accomplish what He came to do.

THE JOURNEY

If you knew you were going to be tortured because people didn't understand you, would you try to explain or defend yourself?

It was evening. Jesus took His disciples to an olive grove to pray. Jesus knew His hour had come. "Please, Father," Jesus agonized, "if there is any way possible that people can be saved without My dying on the cross, let this pass from Me. But most important, let Your will be done, not mine."

Jesus finished praying and returned to the disciples who had all fallen asleep. He had asked them to keep watch and pray, too. But they fell asleep. They had no clue what was about to happen.

Suddenly torches lit up the garden. A detachment of soldiers led by

Judas came toward Jesus. The religious leaders stood in front, wearing a smug look on their faces. They were laughing inwardly at their cleverness of paying one of Jesus' disciples a small amount of money to betray Him.

"Who is it you want?" Jesus asked, knowing they had come for Him.

"Jesus of Nazareth," they stated.

"I am He," Jesus replied. The authority and power of His words made them draw back and fall to the ground. Jesus asked them again, "Who is it you want?" and they gave the same reply. "I told you I am He," Jesus said. Pointing to His disciples, Jesus added, "Let the others go since I am who you want."

Peter couldn't believe what was happening. "No! You can't take Jesus away!" he shouted as he grabbed a sword and struck the ear of the high priest's servant.

Jesus put a stop to it immediately. "Shall I not do what I have come to do?" Jesus said. Then He healed the man's ear.

Jesus allowed Himself to be bound and taken away. All the disciples scattered for fear, just as Jesus had said they would. Peter ran, but then secretly followed along, keeping a safe distance. They led Jesus through a courtyard and to the high priest for a secret trial.

Peter came into the courtyard and stood by the fire where others were warming their hands. He hoped to mix with the group unnoticed. He nervously kept one eye in the direction where they had taken Jesus.

"Hey," a girl said as she saw the flickering light fall upon Peter's face, "you're not one of Jesus' disciples are you?"

"I am not," Peter said nervously. Fear trembled through his body; surely he could be in danger if they discovered he was one of Jesus' disciples. The questions came two more times as others recognized Peter. "No!" Peter lied, "I do not know Him!"

Suddenly a rooster crowed three times and Peter immediately remembered. He had denied Jesus, just as Jesus had said. Peter ran out, his heart torn with grief.

The high priest was still questioning Jesus behind closed doors concerning His disciples and His teachings. "I always spoke openly and said nothing in secret," Jesus replied. "If you ask anyone who has heard Me, they will plainly tell you what I have said."

Suddenly a sharp sting shot across Jesus' face as one of the officials standing nearby slapped Him. "How dare You answer the High Priest in such a way!" he threatened between clenched teeth. "No one of such unimportance should speak to a high priest in such a manner!"

Jesus could have proven He was far greater than any high priest, but didn't. Instead, He patiently answered, "If I have said something wrong, tell Me what I have said. But, if I have spoken the truth, why do you strike Me?"

When morning dawned, Jesus was taken to the palace of the Roman governor. The Jews would not enter the building, but remained outside for fear of becoming ceremonially unclean and not being able to celebrate the Passover.

Pilate came out onto the steps and talked with them there. "What charges do you have against this man?" he asked.

"He's a criminal!" they shouted.

Pilate told them to try Jesus in their own Jewish courts. "But we have no right to execute someone!" they responded. They wanted to be certain Jesus would be put to death.

Pilate returned inside and questioned Jesus. "Are You really King of the Jews? What is it You have done?"

"My Kingdom is not of this world but from another place," Jesus calmly answered. "If My Kingdom were of this world, My servants would be fighting for My release."

"So, You are a king, then!" Pilate replied.

Jesus stated, "You are right in saying I am a king. I came into the world for this reason and to speak truth. Everyone who is on the side of truth follows Me."

CLIMBING ONWARD

Read John 18:11 in your Bible. What do you think this means? What do you think it meant for Jesus? Notice how He set His mind to do what He needed to do out of love for us.

Skill Time

From what you have learned so far, see if you can point to five things that Jesus either said or did that helped prove He was no ordinary man. (Hint: Take a quick review through the other Gospel books if you need to.) Add these things to your ongoing list of what you are learning (or remembering) concerning Jesus.

THAT WAS NO ACCIDENT

TAKEN FROM JOHN 18-19

GETTING READY

As you begin, spend a few minutes in prayer. Search your heart and ask God to help you to see how Jesus' death was no accident.

THE JOURNEY

Would you ever willingly be punished for something you didn't do?

Pilate didn't know what to do with Jesus. "As far as I'm concerned, He has done nothing wrong," Pilate told the crowd. "It is your custom that at Passover I release one prisoner to you. Shall I release to you the 'King of the Jews?' " he asked, fearful of making an unpopular decision.

"No!" they shouted, "Not Him! Release Barabbas!" Barabbas was a criminal worthy of punishment.

Pilate ordered Jesus to be taken away. Jesus was stripped of His clothes and severely beaten. One by one, Jesus endured the stings of the blows as claw-like metal pieces ripped open His skin.

"Hail, King of the Jews!" the soldiers mocked, bowing down before

Him and laughing. They placed a purple robe on Jesus and shoved a crown upon His head, which dug into His skin. They then hit Jesus and spit upon His face.

Wanting to give the crowd one last chance, Pilate brought Jesus out before the crowd. "Here is your king," Pilate offered.

"Crucify Him! Crucify Him!" the crowd shouted.

"Take Him and crucify Him yourself!" Pilate said, "I see nothing wrong with which to charge Him."

"We have a law that He must die, for He claims to be the Son of God," they shouted.

When Pilate heard this, he grew afraid and pulled Jesus to the side. "Where do You come from?" he asked in a panicked voice. When Jesus gave no answer, Pilate demanded, "Why don't You speak to me? Don't You know I have the power to set You free or to crucify You?"

Jesus replied, "The only power you have is that which God allows."

Pilate was torn. "Shall I crucify your King?" he asked the angry mob.

"We have no king but Caesar!" they yelled.

Pilate turned Jesus over to be crucified. Four soldiers led Jesus through the streets. He carried His own cross. Reaching Golgotha, the soldiers drove metal spikes into Jesus' hands and hung Him between two criminals. The soldiers divided up Jesus' clothes, casting lots for His tunic. As they did so, prophecy was being fulfilled. "They divided up my garments . . . and cast lots for my clothing," (Psalm 22:18).

As Jesus hung on the cross, some mocked Him. Others challenged Him to come off the cross and prove His power to save Himself. "He saved others, but He can't save Himself!" they laughed.

Jesus could have proven His power, but would not. He knew that all was completed so the Scriptures would be fulfilled. He looked to heaven and said, "Into Your hands I commit My Spirit. It is finished."

At that instant, the veil in the Temple was miraculously torn in two from top to bottom.

Because the next day was Passover, the Jews asked for the legs of those being crucified to be broken so they could die quickly and be

buried before the Sabbath began. The soldiers broke the legs of the criminals, but noticed Jesus was already dead so they left His legs unbroken.
Wanting to be sure Jesus was dead, a soldier thrust a spear into Jesus'
side and blood and water flowed out. Even in dying, Jesus was in control
and fulfilling details of prophecy: "Not one of His bones will be broken"
(Psalm 34:20) and "they will look on the one they have pierced"
(Zechariah 12:10). Jesus' death was no accident; it was an event planned
by God for a very special purpose.

In your own Bible, read John 19:30. What were
Jesus' words? Do you think He was talking about His life or the payment
for man's sins?

THINKING on your FEET

If someone says, "It's a shame. Jesus
was just a good man who happened to be in the wrong
place at the wrong time and got killed," what would you
say in response?

SEEING IS BELIEVING?

TAKEN FROM JOHN 20

GETTING READY

Take a few minutes to quiet your heart. Thank Jesus for what He has done for you. Ask God to strengthen your faith in Him.

THE JOURNEY

Have you ever doubted your faith? Have you ever asked in the back of your mind, "How can I know for sure I'm right?"

"No! It can't be!" Mary panicked. She had come to the tomb while it was still the last watches of the night. Even in the early morning light, Mary could plainly see something was not right. The tomb had been sealed to make sure no one could enter or exit, yet the stone was rolled away! Unable to bear this bad news alone, Mary ran to tell Peter and John.

"They've taken Jesus out of the tomb," she panted, trying to catch her breath, "and we don't know where they've put Him!" Despair was in her voice. Peter and John immediately began running to the tomb. Mary followed behind them, unable to keep up.

Being the first to reach the tomb, John peered in. He saw the strips of linen Jesus had been wrapped in. No one would steal a body and take the linen off, he thought.

Peter came down the path, pushed past John and went inside the tomb. He was out of breath and wheezing. Looking over at the linens, Peter noticed they were intact—as if the body just evaporated right out of them! Seeing Peter in the tomb, John cautiously stepped in. He saw and then believed, although neither understood how Jesus had risen from the dead. The disciples left and went home.

Finally Mary arrived and was alone at the tomb—or so she thought. Her eyes were puffy and swollen with tears.

"Woman," a voice spoke from behind her, "why do you cry? Who are you looking for?"

Mary didn't turn from the empty tomb. She thought the gardener was speaking. "If you have taken Him away, please tell me where, and I will go get Him," she said between sobs.

Jesus finally said to her, "Mary."

The sound of that voice was strangely wonderful! So full of love and tenderness! She turned toward the voice and looked right into the eyes of Jesus. "Rabboni!" she cried as she reached out to Him.

> The "last watches of the night" were usually 3 AM—6 AM. It was a custom to visit the tomb of someone you loved for three days after they were buried. Since traveling was not permitted on the Sabbath, this was the soonest Mary could come.

"Don't cling to Me, but go tell the others. I have not yet returned to heaven and they will want to see Me too."

Mary took off running; her feet never felt so light and full of speed. Finding the disciples she burst out, "I have seen the Lord!" and began to tell them what Jesus had said to her.

Later that day the disciples were all meeting in the upper room secretly out of fear. The same Jewish authorities who put Jesus to death would no doubt be looking for them, too. They held their breath at the sound of footsteps and every knock at the door. All the disciples were there except Thomas, who wanted to be left alone in his grief.

"Peace be with you," Jesus said as He came and stood in their midst. He showed them His hands and side. His friends were overcome with joy! So it was true! Jesus did rise from the dead! They must tell Thomas!

Thomas was always cautious and slow to believe—but when he did believe something, he believed it with all his heart. "You saw His hands and side, but unless I see and place my finger in the nail marks on His hands, and place my hand in the wound on His side, I will not believe," Thomas replied.

A week had gone by and the disciples were meeting behind locked doors in the upper room again. Thomas joined them this time and Jesus came again just as He had before. "Thomas," Jesus said lovingly, "put your finger here and see My hands. Reach out and put your hand into My side. Stop doubting and believe."

Thomas did as Jesus invited him to do. "My Lord and My God!" Thomas breathed in an almost whisper-like voice filled with love and awe.

"You believe Thomas, because you have seen. Blessed are those who have not seen what you just did, and yet believe," Jesus tenderly replied.

CLIMBING ONWARD

Read John 20:29 in your own Bible. The second sentence is talking about us! What does it say?

Skill Time

Have you ever wondered why the stone was rolled away? God didn't roll the stone away for His own benefit, but for ours. He invites people to see the proof of the empty tomb and believe. Jesus' death and resurrection are a historical fact documented by both Christians and non-Christians. We have the facts written down for us in the Scriptures so that we might know and believe.

Turn to John 20:31 in your own Bible and mark it with a highlighter pen. Read it aloud several times, emphasizing a different word each time you read it. Think about what you are reading and memorize the verse. God is never alarmed about your doubts and fears. Tell Him about the things you are struggling with, and ask Him to help you grow in your faith.

BUT WHAT ABOUT . . . ?

TAKEN FROM JOHN 21

GETTING READY

Spend a few moments talking to God. Ask Him to examine your heart and help you to love and follow Jesus all the more.

THE JOURNEY

Do you find it hard to do what you're supposed to do because you're distracted by what other people are or aren't doing?

"Nothing! Plain old nothing!" Peter grunted as they pulled in the nets. They had been fishing all night. Now it was morning and they had nothing to show for all their work. Not one fish! It was embarrassing.

"Friends," a voice called from shore, "try throwing your net on the right side of the boat!"

The disciples looked at one another. It was not uncommon for people standing up on shore to see fish in the clear water. Oftentimes fishermen would have a helper who stood on shore and called out directions regarding where to throw the net. The disciples were so discouraged they were willing to listen to any advice. They did as the stranger said.

Suddenly, there was a tug at the net and the boat tilted with the

111

weight of the fish! John looked up at the stranger on the shore and said, "It is the Lord!"

Peter jerked his head up and looked with excitement. He wanted to be the first to greet the Lord so he quickly put on his tunic, and jumped into the water to swim to the Lord. The others followed along in the boat, dragging the fish behind them.

Arriving on the shore, they saw a fire burning with the sweet smell of fish and bread. "Come and have breakfast," Jesus said.

After the meal, Jesus turned to Peter and asked, "Peter, do you love me more than these?"

Peter looked at the other disciples. He remembered how he had bragged about loving Jesus more than they, and his bold statement of willingness to die for Jesus, even if everyone else denied Him. "Yes, Lord," Peter said uncomfortably, "You know I love You!"

"Peter," Jesus said a second time, "do you really love Me?" Peter closed his eyes for a moment. He wanted to blot out the memory of hearing the rooster crow three times and the terrible event of denying his Lord. Again, he answered, "Yes Lord, You know I love You!"

According to Jewish law, it was considered a religious act to offer someone a greeting, and no religious act could be done unless a person was fully clothed. Wanting to be the first to greet Jesus, Peter put on his outer tunic then jumped in the water.

Jesus then looked deep into Peter's eyes and lovingly asked for the third time, "Do you love Me?"

Peter felt hurt in his heart and met Jesus' gaze. "Lord, You know everything," he said longingly, "You know that I love You."

"Then feed my sheep," Jesus said tenderly.

Not only did Jesus forgive Peter for denying Him, but He trusted Peter with a job to do! Peter was to take care of other believers who were Jesus' flock of sheep. Jesus continued on, explaining to Peter how he would be used by God and how he would eventually die. Then Jesus said, "Follow Me." Those words were strangely familiar, for they were the same words Jesus used when He first called Peter to be one of His disciples.

Peter's heart leapt within him, then a quick, panicked feeling struck. "Lord, but what about him?" Peter curiously asked while pointing to John.

"Whatever John does or does not do, what difference does that make to you?" Jesus questioned. "You must follow Me for yourself, regardless of what other people think or do," Jesus said to Peter.

Read John 21:21 in your own Bible. Read it, substituting your name for Peter, and the name of someone who distracts you after the words: "Lord, and what about . . ." Skip down to verse 22 and read the last eight or nine words.

DANGER AHEAD

You will be tempted to keep your eyes on others and measure yourself by what they do or don't do. Don't! Your walk and relationship with God depends on no one else but you. With your eyes on the Lord and your Bible as your guide, journey with Him. Don't worry if others follow.

GETTING YOUR BEARINGS:
THE BOOK OF ACTS

Acts is an exciting book full of history and background. It helps us see exactly what happened after Jesus rose from the dead and returned to heaven. In Acts we see the beginning of the Church, the missionary journeys of Paul and Peter, and other exciting events!

Acts was written by Luke–the same person who also wrote the Gospel of Luke. The first verse of Acts opens where Luke closes in his Gospel, almost like a "part two" of the story. In the Gospels we see Jesus dying for our sins. In Acts we see Him very much alive and being glorified in heaven. In the Gospels we learn about Jesus' teachings and in Acts we see the results of those teachings. We see what Jesus continues to do in and through the lives of His followers.

As you journey through Acts, keep your eyes open for events and names of the different places Paul visited on his three missionary journeys. You will see those names again as you continue your journey through the New Testament. Above all, enjoy your journey through the wonderful book of Acts! This book is like a giant puzzle board into which all the other pieces of the New Testament fit.

DO WHAT!

TAKEN FROM ACTS 1

GETTING READY

As you prepare your heart for today's journey into God's Word, ask the Lord to challenge you. Give Him permission to point out what needs to be changed in your life.

THE JOURNEY

What do you do when you're told to do something and you don't know how to begin?

The silence was awkward as the disciples looked at one another. For the past forty days since Jesus had risen from the dead, He had been appearing to His disciples. Jesus talked with them, ate with them, and even let them see and touch His scars. He continued teaching about the Kingdom of God so they could be sure it was Him. For forty days He had come and gone, but today something was very different.

"Don't leave Jerusalem. Wait here for the gift I talked about and that which My Father promised to send to you," Jesus instructed the disciples.

The disciples weren't sure what this meant. "Are You going to bring the kingdom back to Israel now?" they asked.

Jesus kindly corrected them and gave them a challenge. "It is not for you to be concerned about God's timing on such things," He said. "Instead, you will receive power when the Holy Spirit comes upon you. You will be My witnesses not only in Jerusalem, Judea, and Samaria, but also to the very ends of the earth," Jesus said.

When Jesus finished speaking those words, He was taken up toward heaven. The disciples stood watching until they could no longer see Jesus in the clouds. They were speechless and amazed. Jesus wanted them to go and tell others the good news of God's kingdom, yet they were supposed to wait. They were to be His witnesses, telling what they knew and experienced personally, but they were not permitted to go anywhere yet. What was the gift Jesus talked about? How would they know when they had received it? All of these questions kept going through their minds as they looked up into the sky, straining to see Jesus.

Houses were built with smaller rooms on the main floor to support larger, upper rooms on the top floor. These upper rooms were places where larger groups would commonly meet.

Suddenly two men dressed in white asked the disciples, "Why are you standing here looking into the sky? Do you not know this same Jesus who went into heaven on a cloud will come back in the same manner as He said?"

After hearing this, the disciples left the Mount of Olives and returned to Jerusalem. When they arrived, they went to the upper room where they had been staying and meeting together. All eleven of the disciples were there, as well as Jesus' brothers, His mother, Mary, and other women who were His followers. At first there was an awkward silence and an uncertainty as to what they should do next. Should they make special plans? Should they divide themselves up into teams and map out the areas surrounding them? Should they all stay together as one group? How would they go about this task Jesus gave them to do? Rather than worry and figure out their own plans, the disciples decided to do God's work in God's way. Before they did anything else, they prayed together and waited for the help Jesus promised to send.

CLIMBING ONWARD

Look up Acts 1:8 in your Bible. What two things did Jesus say would happen to the disciples? Skip down to verse 14. What was their response?

THINKING on your FEET

You have a big task and you don't know where to begin. What will your first move be?

SPECIAL DELIVERY

TAKEN FROM ACTS 2

GETTING READY

Before you journey into God's Word today, spend some time talking with Him. Ask God to help you understand the strength that He offers, and how it can take you beyond your own abilities.

THE JOURNEY

What goes through your mind when you see friends suddenly do something they wouldn't or couldn't do before?

It was the celebration of Pentecost. It was one of three festivals that every Jewish male living within twenty miles of Jerusalem had to attend. The streets of Jerusalem were full of people and buzzing with activity.

During this celebration the disciples were still praying and waiting for Jesus to send the promised gift to them. Before going back to heaven, Jesus had told the disciples to wait in Jerusalem. He had mentioned they would receive power when the Holy Spirit came upon them. So far, nothing had happened. The disciples met constantly to pray and even selected another apostle named Matthias to take Judas's place (the one who betrayed Jesus). The number of Jesus' disciples had now grown, and 120 were all meeting together in one place.

Suddenly, a loud rush of wind came down from heaven and swirled about them. They all looked up in surprise. *What could this be?* they thought as they looked about in wonder and awe. What seemed to be flames of fire could be seen resting above the head of each one in the room. The apostles couldn't help but think back to Moses and how God used a pillar of fire to guide the Israelites and show His presence to them—just as He was now showing His presence to all those in that room.

A *disciple* may be any believer and follower of Jesus Christ. *Apostle* (meaning "sent one") was the term given first to the twelve disciples who were sent out by Jesus to carry on His work. The first apostles (except Paul) were eyewitnesses of Jesus and were trained by Him. We usually use the word apostle for the twelve disciples and Paul, but sometimes the New Testament stretches it to cover other missionaries.

As the Spirit of God rested on each one, he or she began to speak in different languages. This was the gift Jesus had promised! They were all baptized into the Holy Spirit. The Holy Spirit would comfort, guide, and enable them to do God's will. What joy! What power! What a surprise!

People on the street heard this noise and stopped to listen. Many understood what was being said, for the language was in their own native tongue! They were amazed and wondered, "What does this mean?"

Some, however, made fun of the disciples. Laughing they said, "They've had too much wine to drink!"

Hearing that comment, Peter rose to speak to the crowd. He was no longer a coward afraid to stand up for Jesus.

"Listen to what I have to say," Peter boldly spoke, as he began to explain what the people were seeing and hearing. "These men are not drunk," Peter defended, "it is only nine in the morning! What you see and hear is what the prophet Joel spoke about!" The crowd listened as Peter continued. Peter boldly told how Jesus was and still is the Messiah, how He backed His words up with His actions, and how He was approved by God. Peter told how Jesus fulfilled prophecies, how His dying on the cross was no accident, and how Jesus' resurrection was proof of His claims about Himself. "Let everyone be sure of this," Peter challenged, "you may have crucified Jesus, but God raised Him from the dead, and made Him to be both Lord and Christ."

When the people heard this, their hearts were pierced. "What shall we do?"

Peter answered simply and powerfully. "Repent and be baptized in the name of Jesus Christ for the forgiveness of your sins!" Those who heard and received Peter's powerful message were baptized, and about 3,000 people were added to Jesus' followers that day!

CLIMBING ONWARD

Open your Bible to the second chapter of Acts. Read the last sentence (verse 47). What does it say? Read it again, emphasizing the word *Lord*.

CROSS ROADS

When counting on your strength or God's, which do you think is more dependable and gets better results? Why?

HE'S CHANGED

TAKEN FROM ACTS 4

GETTING READY

Before you journey through today's lesson, spend a few minutes talking to God. Ask Him to help you understand the power He has to change lives.

THE JOURNEY

Do you know anyone who has changed so much it makes others stand back and say, "Wow! What happened?"

"I tell you," the religious leaders sneered, "if you continue to preach about Jesus, you will regret the day you were ever born!"

"Yes," threatened one of the members of the Sanhedrin, "don't you remember we have the power to deliver you over to the Romans to die, or did you forget the death of your Jesus already?"

Peter stood by, unflinching. The one threatening him was right in his face and Peter could feel his hot and heavy breath. Peter and John were being examined by the Sanhedrin as a result of a wonderful miracle God did through them. In Jesus' name, they had healed a man who had been born lame.

As Peter stood there listening to the threats of what would happen if they didn't stop preaching about Jesus, he couldn't help but think about his Lord. It seemed just yesterday, yet so long ago, that Jesus Himself stood trial before these very men. Peter's mind raced back to Jesus' loving response to his once prideful boasting. "I'll never deny you Lord," Peter had said, "even if everyone else falls away!" Peter closed his eyes as he recalled the rooster crowing three times when he denied Jesus. What a coward he had been to deny the One who loved him so very much. But all that was in the past now. Jesus had personally forgiven Peter and then given him a special job to do. Not only that, the power of the Holy Spirit was present for Peter and the disciples to rely on. Peter was no longer the same as he had been before. He now had a boldness and power that amazed even himself!

The Sadducees didn't believe in angels or the resurrection. It has been said, "That is why they were SAD, YOU SEE!"

"Have we made ourselves clear?" the voice said, snapping Peter back to reality.

Peter looked over at John who was also being threatened, and then Peter spoke for them both. "Judge for yourselves whether it is right in God's eyes for us to obey you rather than God. As for us, we cannot and will not stop speaking about that which we have seen and heard."

The members of the Sanhedrin were angered but realized there was nothing more they could do, so they released Peter and John.

Rejoining the other believers, Peter and John reported what had happened to them as well as the threats that were made. After hearing this, the believers united together in prayer. They did not ask to be removed from their problems, but instead thanked God that He was in control!

"Lord, you know of these threats against us. Help us to continue speaking out boldly in your name," they prayed. As they prayed, the place where they were meeting began to shake, and they were all filled with the Holy Spirit's power.

CLIMBING ONWARD

In your Bible, read Acts 4:29. Do you think the threats bothered Peter and John? What did they ask God to do?

Skill Time

Peter and John were transformed, having been with Jesus and empowered by God's Spirit. They knew in whom and what they believed and were willing to stand on that fact. Look up Acts 4:12 in your Bible and read it, emphasizing the word "no" each time you see it. Read it several more times and memorize the verse. This is solid ground on which to stand, and it's the very fact Peter and John stood on.

CRIME DOESN'T PAY

TAKEN FROM ACTS 5

GETTING READY

Take a few minutes to quiet your thoughts. Tell God what is on your heart. Ask Him to help you understand what is on His.

THE JOURNEY

Do you have a friend who acts one way at church to impress others, but lives something completely different? Why do you think he or she acts this way?

Great things were happening in the group of believers. Even though they heard the warnings and threats of what would happen if they continued to speak out about Jesus, they stood firm. God stood with them and blessed them beyond measure. Such a spirit a love and unity was among the believers who willingly shared what they had with those in need. The new believers considered themselves to be brothers and sisters with one another. Barnabas was one such example. His real name was Joseph, but the apostles renamed him Barnabas (meaning "Son of encouragement"), for he had a way of encouraging others.

One day, Barnabas sold some land he owned and brought the money in for the group. "This is for the needs of others," he said as he laid the money at the apostles' feet. No one had asked him to do this; he did it out of his love for the Lord and a willingness to help other believers.

Ananias and his wife Sapphira saw Barnabas's example and the praise he received. They wanted a little glory and praise for themselves, so they went and sold the land they owned. (Doing the right thing for the wrong reason started the ball rolling.)

"Why should we give all the money we earned," reasoned Ananias, "when we can keep some for ourselves and just say we brought it all?"

Striking Ananias and Sapphira dead seems to be harsh discipline, but God used it to make a point and set an example. In the Old Testament, Achan (Joshua 7: 25, 26) was stoned to death for hiding stolen goods in his tent.

"That's a great idea!" Sapphira agreed, "No one will ever know!" Together they planned what they would say, and agreed how much they would keep back for themselves.

The next day, Ananias rose early and spent some extra time getting himself ready. He wanted to look his best for the great impression he was going to make on the others. *Wait until they see what I have to share with the group,* he thought proudly. He felt smug about his and Sapphira's little secret.

Just as Barnabas had done, Ananias came and laid his money at the apostles' feet and announced, "The Lord spoke to me and told me to sell my field and bring in all the money to help other believers in need." He waited for a response, but did not get the reaction he expected.

"Ananias," Peter replied, "how is it that Satan has so filled your heart? What made you do this? You have lied, saying the Holy Spirit told you to do something He didn't tell you to do. And you have lied in keeping back some of the money for yourself while claiming to give all! You have not lied to men but to God Himself."

Those words struck Ananias's heart and God struck Ananias dead. The group standing around fell silent and were in fear. God demanded that they be pure of heart and would not tolerate dishonesty. Ananias was taken away and buried.

Three hours later Sapphira walked in. Perhaps she expected a grand welcoming for the great thing she and Ananias had done. Not knowing what had happened to Ananias, she didn't get the reaction she'd expected.

"Tell me," Peter began, "is this the price you and Ananias got for selling your land?"

Sapphira didn't hesitate. "Yes, that is the price," she lied.

Peter replied, "Have you agreed to lie? You are testing God's Holy Spirit to see how much you can get away with before He judges. Look! The men who buried your husband will carry your body out as well."

Sapphira fell at Peter's feet and the men carried her body out and buried her next to her husband.

CLIMBING ONWARD

In your Bible, read Acts 5:4. Read the last sentence again. This is pretty serious stuff!

DANGER AHEAD

Lying to God (who knows your thoughts anyway) is a serious thing. Love and serve Him with your whole heart. Don't pretend to give Him all while holding back.

WE'RE BAAACK!

TAKEN FROM ACTS 5

GETTING READY

Stop and pray. Ask God to help you understand the importance of obeying Him.

THE JOURNEY

Laws are for us to obey, but should you obey man's law when it demands you disobey God's laws?

Solomon's Colonnade was a large porch on the East side of the Temple where all the believers of Jesus met. Since word of Ananias and Sapphira's fate had spread, people were more cautious about joining the believers. They didn't want the same thing to happen to them because they were halfhearted about the things of God. As a result, the believers (now called the Church) were protected from hypocrites and pretenders, and God was daily increasing the number of those who truly believed.

Miracles occurred often, and people stood in awe as they recognized something special. Because the believers met at a public place on the Temple grounds, large crowds could see the great things God was doing. Peter and the apostles held great respect in the people's eyes.

When the members of the Sanhedrin saw this popularity, they grew jealous and fearful. Such a large following could cause an uprising, and the Roman government would step in and no longer let the Sanhedrin govern the people. They didn't want this, so they arrested all the apostles and put them in jail.

During the night, an angel of the Lord opened the jail doors and set the apostles free. "Go and continue to preach in the Temple courts," the angel instructed.

The apostles set out to do just that. At daybreak, the apostles entered the Temple area and began to teach the people about Jesus, just as the angel had instructed.

> "Flogging" was the beating of a person with a stick or a whip. The legal and allowable limit was forty beatings. The apostles were beaten forty times less one so as not to break the law.

Meanwhile, the high priest and his helpers called together the Sanhedrin, and they sent officers to the jail to get the apostles.

Moments later, the officers returned. "We found the jail locked and undisturbed," they fearfully reported. "Even the guards were still standing there. But when we opened the doors, the apostles were gone!" The captain of the temple guard and the chief priest were puzzled. What had happened to the apostles?

Suddenly, a messenger burst into the room. "You won't believe this," he said trying to catch his breath, "but the same men you had thrown in jail are back, and they're teaching people in the Temple courts again!"

The chief priest and members of the Sanhedrin were speechless. So, they thought, our guards are carefully guarding jail cells that are empty, and we stand here ready to judge prisoners we don't even have! If this isn't bad enough, they are outside at this very moment preaching in the Temple courts under our very nose!

The Temple captain left with some of his officers and shortly returned with the apostles. For fear of their popularity with the crowds, they had been gathered up without force. The high priest fired out questions one after another. He had such a distaste for the apostles and

Jesus that he wouldn't even say Jesus' name. "We warned you not to teach in that name!" he hissed.

Peter and the others simply replied, "We must obey God rather than men!"

Peter then spoke, accusing them. "You killed Jesus, but God raised Him from the dead." Peter went on to explain how they could have forgiveness of sins if they repented.

Gamaliel was a member of the Sanhedrin and an expert in Jewish law. The apostle Paul had studied under Gamaliel.

The religious leaders were furious and ready to have the apostles killed. At this point a Pharisee named Gamaliel stood and spoke. His words calmed the angered Sanhedrin. "Carefully consider what you do with these men. If what they do is of men, it will die out on its own. But if what they do is of God and you try to stop it, you would be fighting God Himself." As a result of this counsel, the officers had the apostles flogged and ordered them once again not to speak in the name of Jesus.

The apostles left the Sanhedrin rejoicing because they had been counted worthy to suffer for Jesus' name. Day after day, in the Temple courts and from house to house the apostles continued teaching and proclaiming the Good News about Jesus.

CLIMBING ONWARD

In your Bible, look up Acts 5:29. Notice Peter didn't say "we would like to," but rather, "we must." Must what?

CROSS ROADS

If forced to choose, will you stand with God or will you stand against Him?

NOTHING PERSONAL

TAKEN FROM ACTS 6-8

GETTING READY

Spend a few moments in prayer. Thank God for the freedoms you have and give God permission to do as He pleases with them.

THE JOURNEY

How do you react when someone picks on you just because you're a Christian?

Five-thousand believers now followed Jesus, and the Church was growing daily. There were many different backgrounds within the group. Some of the Jews who had always lived in Palestine were called Hebrews and spoke Aramaic. They started to look down on the Greek speaking Jews who had lived outside the land. These people were neglected when it came time to share with one another.

Peter and the apostles solved the problem by appointing seven men who took charge of handing out the money and food being shared. With the help of these seven men, the apostles could continue devoting their time to praying and proclaiming Jesus. The men chosen were to be full of wisdom and controlled by the Holy Spirit's power. The first two names selected were those of Stephen and Philip.

Stephen was well-loved by many. Not only kind, Stephen was wise, and had a great ability to speak out for the Lord. God did great wonders and miraculous signs through Stephen. One day, a group of men didn't like Stephen's message and began to argue with him. When they couldn't stand up to his wisdom and the power of his message, they got angry.

"We heard Stephen speaking against Moses and God!" they lied. They secretly convinced others to spread these lied about Stephen. In no time, Stephen was brought before the Sanhedrin to be examined.

"This man doesn't stop speaking against the temple and against the Law," they falsely accused. "We heard him say Jesus would destroy this temple and change the laws Moses handed down to us," they argued. Hate-filled eyes turned toward Stephen. The temple was sacred and because it held such a high place in the religious leader's hearts, they often made the mistake of worshipping it.

Jesus never claimed to destroy the temple; He had said, "when you destroy this temple (My body), I will raise it up again on the third day." As for Moses' laws, Jesus came to fulfill them, and that would bring a new law into effect. What Stephen said was correct and true. The fault was not in him, but in those who heard and twisted his message.

The Sanhedrin looked at Stephen and waited for him to reply. They couldn't help but notice his face looked almost like that of an angel. "Are these charges true?" the high priest demanded.

Instead of defending himself, Stephen began with a brief history lesson. He reminded then how God called out Abraham, then Moses to lead the people in a way they were not used to going. He told how Israel rebelled against God and made a calf out of gold. He even spoke about Solomon building the temple, proclaiming it as a symbol of God's presence and not God's home.

Stephen continued on, "You stiff-necked people! You are just like your fathers who resisted God and even killed the prophets who predicted the coming of the righteous One!"

The Sanhedrin gnashed their teeth in a fit of anger after hearing these words. Hatred filled their eyes, but Stephen didn't notice. He seemed to look beyond them and saw Jesus standing at the right hand of God, as if to welcome him into heaven. "I see heaven opened," Stephen reported, "and Jesus standing at the right hand of God!"

Stoning was a common form of capital punishment. After two hearings to determine someone's guilt, the person was taken to a cliff and thrown down by those testifying against him. If he lived, big boulders and stones were then thrown down upon him.

The Sanhedrin would listen to no more. Covering their ears with their hands, they rushed upon Stephen, dragged him out the city, and stoned him. As Stephen was being killed, he looked toward heaven and repeated the words of His Savior, "Father, forgive them please. . . ." With those words on his lips, Stephen died.

A religious leader named Saul watched the stoning as he guarded the clothes of those stoning Stephen. Saul agreed with everything he saw. Little did he know what effect this would have on his life later.

CLIMBING ONWARD

In your own Bible, read Acts 8:1-4. what happened as a result of Stephen's death? Stephen knew he was being put to death by people who opposed God's plan, yet He knew God was still in control.

Skill Time

In other countries at this very hour and minute, Christians are being put to death for their faith in Christ. The only charge against them is that they know and follow Jesus—in some countries that is against the law. With the freedoms we enjoy, it is hard to believe this activity happens. Right now, take a few quiet minutes and pray for fellow believers in other countries and thank God for their lives. Ask God to give them strength to stand for Him as Stephen did. Ask God to give you the same courage if you were ever called upon to do the same.

CAN I JOIN YOU?

TAKEN FROM ACTS 8

GETTING READY

Stop and pray before you journey into God's Word. Thank the Lord that He is in control over the circumstances in your life and that nothing just happens by chance.

THE JOURNEY

Have you ever seen something happen and you knew it wasn't by chance or coincidence?

Philip continued traveling in Samaria and proclaiming Jesus. On one such trip, an angel sent from God appeared before Philip. "Go south and take the desert road running from Jerusalem to Gaza," the angel said.

Even though this was an unusual request, Philip obeyed God's angel and started out for the road he was told to travel. . . .

Down the road, Philip saw a royal chariot belonging to an Ethiopian queen. It carried a man in charge of all the queen's riches. The man was travelling from Jerusalem, where he had worshiped, to his home in Africa. He had become weary of trying to please all the gods his people worshiped. He wanted to know about the one true God of the Jews.

"Go over to that chariot and stay near it," the Holy Spirit directed Philip.

Philip did not hesitate. As he ran up to the chariot, he heard the man reading aloud from the prophet Isaiah.

"Do you understand what you are reading?" Philip asked in a humble voice.

The man looked down from the chariot and studied Philip for a moment. The word help was written all over the man's face. "How can I understand this unless someone explains it to me?" he said as he invited Philip to join him in the chariot.

"Tell me," he questioned, "when it says 'He was led like a sheep to the slaughter, and as a lamb before the shearer is silent, so He did not open His mouth. In His humiliation He was deprived of justice,' is the prophet speaking about himself or someone else?"

Baptism is an outward action, showing others you identify with Christ, proclaiming your loyalty to Jesus.

Philip not only answered the man's question, but also used that very passage of Scripture to explain the good news of Jesus who had fulfilled those prophecies.

As they passed by a section of water, the man said, "Look, what keeps me from being baptized?"

Philip saw the sincerity in the man's eyes. It would be very unusual to baptize this man who was neither Jew nor Samaritan. Yet, the chances of traveling on a road in the middle of the desert and meeting a non-Jewish man who happened to be reading the Scriptures and wanting an explanation made it obvious to Philip that God was at work.

The chariot was ordered to a halt and both Philip and the man climbed out. Right there, alongside the road, Philip baptized this new believer in Jesus. What joy surrounded the event!

As the men came up out of the water, the Spirit of the Lord suddenly took Philip away. The man he baptized continued to his homeland, rejoicing, and Philip went on to the other things God prepared for him to do. . . .

CLIMBING ONWARD

Look up Acts 8:35 in your Bible and read it. What did Philip do according to this verse? How did he do it? Notice how Philip started where the man was at and at the man's level of interest. With love, gentleness, and dependence upon the Holy Spirit, Philip was able to explain things and lead the man into a relationship with Christ.

Skill Time

This week look for opportunities to find where someone is at spiritually and to lead them onward to Christ. Simply ask God to use you; then be ready, obedient, and sensitive to God's leading. (Also, it might be helpful to review the salvation Scriptures on the last page of this book!)

PRESTO - CHANGE-O!

TAKEN FROM ACTS 9

GETTING READY

Spend some time preparing your heart. Examine your life—where you've been and where you're headed. Ask God to help you see how His love for you is not based upon your performance.

THE JOURNEY

What do you think when you hear someone say, "I've done too many bad things for God to love me"?

"So they think they've gotten away, do they?", Saul muttered to himself as he went to the high priest for legal papers. He was a Pharisee who would have nothing to do with this Jesus nonsense. Saul had gleefully stood by and watched a believer named Stephen being stoned to death. *Imagine*, Saul thought to himself, *someone making such blasphemous claims about a man named Jesus!*

Saul quickened his step. Having heard that some believers had escaped to Damascus, he was determined to go there and drag them back so they could be killed. The papers from the high priest ordered the synagogue rulers to help him find these people.

The road to Damascus from Jerusalem would be a six– to eight–day journey. Accompanying Saul on this journey were officers of the Sanhedrin—police of sorts. Because Saul was a Pharisee, he could have nothing to do with these men. Saul walked alone, with lots of time to think. He thought of the Christians he had killed. All the Christians he slaughtered had died with such bravery. Stephen's last words asking forgiveness for his enemies haunted Saul's memory. Saul shook his head violently and with great anger. He was a Pharisee—a protector of the Jewish law. If the message Stephen spoke was true, then the beloved Jewish law was in danger. "No!" Saul breathed with hatred. He would fight to the very last ounce of his strength to stop these Christians!

> Ananias was the first person to call Saul "a Christian brother." He is no relation to the Ananias of Acts 5.

The last stretch of road to Damascus went up Mount Hermon. Damascus was nestled in the green valley below. Saul smiled to himself; soon he would have those Christians who had escaped! "They will get what's rightfully coming to them," he sneered as his hatred drove him onward.

Out of nowhere, a blinding flash came down from heaven. Saul caught a glimpse of Jesus standing before him. Then Saul went blind.

"Saul, Saul," Jesus said, "Why are you persecuting Me?"

The voice was loud and clear to Saul, but the travelers with him heard only a loud noise. They couldn't understand what was being said.

"Who are you?," Saul asked as he covered his eyes. The bright light had made them burn painfully.

"I am Jesus, whom you are persecuting," Jesus replied.

Saul fell to his knees and Jesus instructed him to go into the city and wait to be told what to do next.

Saul picked himself up off the ground, but when he opened his eyes, he found he could not see. Instead of marching triumphantly for the kill into Damascus, Saul would be led humbly like a little child. For three days Saul did not eat, drink, or see anything.

Ananias was a disciple who lived in Damascus. Ananias was told by the Lord to visit a certain house and ask for Saul. "But Lord!," Ananias replied, "You don't understand all the bad things this man has done to us Christians! The reason he is here in Damascus is to kill even more!"

But the Lord answered Ananias, "Do as I say, for this man is a chosen instrument of mine. He will carry My name before the Gentiles and their kings, as well as the people of Israel."

Ananias did as God instructed and went to the house. Finding Saul, he placed his hands on him and called him "brother". Ananias explained how Jesus had sent him there. As he explained this, something like scales fell from Saul's eyes and he rose up a changed man.

Saul stayed with the disciples in Damascus and began to preach in the synagogues the very message he had once sought to destroy!

Tarsus was a Greek city and capital of the Cilicia region. It was also Paul's home town.

Saul's rapid change confused the non-believing Jews living in Damascus. "He is proving that Jesus is the Christ by his very life!" they worried, and they plotted to kill Saul. Guards were posted at every gate to keep Saul from escaping. Saul learned of their plans and escaped over the city wall in a basket with the help of believers.

Saul then returned to Jerusalem and tried to join the disciples there, but they would have nothing to do with him. "Perhaps this is one of his many tricks," they said, eyeing him suspiciously. It wasn't until Barnabas came forward and defended Saul that they listened.

Finally being accepted, Saul boldly proclaimed Christ in Jerusalem and went to the very group Stephen had been trying to reach before he was stoned to death. Being a skilled debater himself, Saul left these hostile Jews speechless, and they in their anger sought to kill him as they had Stephen. When the believers in Jerusalem heard this, they took Saul to Caesarea and sent him off to Tarsus.

CLIMBING ONWARD

Open your Bible to chapter 9 of Acts. Read verses 21, 22. Notice anything special? Jesus was able to turn the bad in Saul's life into proof—proof of who Jesus is and what He can do.

DANGER AHEAD

You will run into people who make excuses, saying they've done too many bad things for God to love them. Don't believe it; God doesn't.

IT CAN'T BE—CAN IT?

TAKEN FROM ACTS 12

GETTING READY

Stop and think before you pray today. Prayer is not getting God to bless what we want to do, but it's how we get our hearts in line with what God is doing and the blessings that follow! Ask God to realign your heart by helping you to grow in your personal prayer life.

THE JOURNEY

Have you ever prayed for something impossible and were surprised when your prayers were answered?

It was dark and the metal cuffs on the chains cut into Peter's hands. On either side slept two guards who were handcuffed to Peter. Guards stood watch at the door. King Herod, who had just beheaded James, ordered Peter to be locked in prison to await the same fate. James was the first apostle to be killed. Peter, it seemed, would soon be the second.

Peter sat quietly in the prison and thought. Herod wanted to win favor with the Jews; Jews who chose not to repent and believe in Jesus. There was a growing hatred toward the church in Jerusalem, and any Jew who became a follower of Jesus was despised. The killing of James pleased the rebellious Jews so much that Herod wanted Peter killed. Herod figured that would increase his popularity even more.

Peter looked over at the guards chained to him, then slowly Peter drifted off to sleep. Peter knew God was in control, and he would trust God with his life as well as his death.

In the darkness of the cell, an angel suddenly appeared. The cuffs slipped out. Peter couldn't tell if this was a dream or really happening! The angel motioned for Peter to follow and they quietly slipped past the guards and right out of the door!

Who's who? Herod the Great reigned during the time Jesus was born. He met the wise men and later had the Jewish babies killed. Herod Antipas (great-grandson of Herod the Great) murdered John the Baptist and was the ruler who questioned Jesus. Herod Agrippa (Herod Antipas's nephew) ruled during this time in Acts. He beheaded James.

The air shocked Peter into reality. *"I'm really not dreaming! God sent an angel to rescue me!"* he thought. Peter quickly made his way to Mary's house. Many believers were inside praying for Peter.

Peter quietly knocked on the door. "Who is it?" a servant girl named Rhoda asked.

Standing outside, hoping not to be seen, Peter announced who he was in a hushed voice.

Rhoda recognized Peter's voice and became so excited she left him standing outside while she ran to tell the others. "Peter! It's Peter! He's at the door!" she exclaimed.

The believers gave Rhoda a pitiful look. "That's impossible, Rhoda, you are just overly tired and imagining things," said one.

Another said, "Poor, Peter. It's probably his angel!" As Rhoda kept insisting she was telling the truth, Peter kept knocking on the door. When they finally opened the door and saw Peter, they were amazed and began talking at once! This was an unexpected answer to their prayers! Motioning for them to quiet down, Peter described how the Lord had miraculously brought him out of the prison.

Herod was furious (the next day) when he discovered Peter had escaped! Nothing could stop Peter from proclaiming the Gospel.

CLIMBING ONWARD

In your own Bible, look up Acts 12:14-16 and read it. Reread verse 16. How does it describe the reaction of the believers who had been praying?

Skill Time

God does answer prayer. He invites us to talk with Him and tell Him all our concerns. God has a perfect plan, and He knows how He'll work things out. You can personally see God's faithfulness by keeping track of how He has answered your prayers. Find a notebook and write down your prayer requests. As the Lord answers them, write down the date they were answered and a brief sentence telling how they were answered. Remember, God doesn't always say yes to our requests. Sometimes He answers with a no or sometimes we have to wait.

IT'S NOT THAT BAD

TAKEN FROM ACTS 15

GETTING READY

Before you journey into God's Word today, thank Him for who He is. Ask God to help you see how only He can make a good thing out of a bad situation.

THE JOURNEY

Do you know of a time when God used something negative to bring about something good?

Paul and Barnabas were back home in the Antioch church, reporting about their first missionary journey. It was wonderful news, and everyone rejoiced to hear what God had done through them.

While there was rejoicing, some believers came from Jerusalem with news that was not good; in fact, it was insulting. "You cannot be true believers like us unless you live by the law of Moses and become circumcised," they said. They were looking down on the Antioch believers and trying to place new and harsh religious rules on them. These rules came from Jewish religious traditions, not from Jesus.

Paul was angered and a sharp argument arose. God had proven once that He accepted these believers by giving them His Holy Spirit. Was that not enough proof? Were the Jewish believers in Jerusalem now going to reject those whom God had accepted? *May it never be!* thought Paul as he set off with Barnabas to see the apostles and elders in Jerusalem concerning this matter.

When they arrived in Jerusalem, Paul was welcomed by the church, and he reported God's work among the Gentiles. Some of the Pharisees who were believers replied, "The Gentiles must be circumcised and made to obey the law of Moses or they are not true believers!" So the elders and apostles all discussed this question.

Peter was at the meeting too. He stood to speak in behalf of the Gentiles. "It is through the grace of our Lord Jesus that we have been saved, not by keeping our own laws. In just the same manner, it is by the grace of our Lord Jesus that the Gentiles have been saved as well!"

Next, the assembly listened silently as Paul described the wonders and signs God had done among the Gentiles. The counsel decided not to make the Gentile (non-Jewish) Christians obey all the laws of the Jews. Instead, they came up with a few simple rules for them to follow. They wrote a letter, stating this fact, and apologized for those who had gone without their approval and caused such grief. The matter had been settled, and the Christians did not have to become Jews.

Not long after that, Paul said to Barnabas, "Let's go back and visit the churches in Galatia to see how they are doing." Barnabas agreed and wanted to take his cousin Mark along, but Paul disagreed. "He deserted us on our first missionary trip!" Paul could feel the anger and disappointment surface just by thinking about it. A feeling of disgust stuck in his throat as he flatly stated, "Mark has no part in this ministry and will not be coming along!"

Paul and Barnabas could not agree, so they each went their own separate way. Paul took Silas (one of the Jerusalem messengers) with him and set off for Galatia, strengthening the churches and proclaiming God's Word along the way. Barnabas took Mark and went to Barnabas's homeland of Cyprus.

CLIMBING ONWARD

In your Bible, read Acts 15:39. Notice Mark was taken to Barnabas's homeland of Cyprus. What do you think happened to them? Perhaps Barnabas's encouragement saved Mark for future ministry. Notice a change: turn to II Timothy 4:11 and see what Paul later says about Mark.

DANGER AHEAD

Don't be discouraged by what appear to be hopeless circumstances. God is still in control. For instance: because of the Jerusalem council, Gentile believers were now free from the bonds of Jewish law and were able to worship God and become the true Christian church. Because of the split between Paul and Barnabas, two missionary teams were now available instead of just one.

Sometimes God uses difficulties in our lives to bring about greater results. Trust Him that He knows what He is doing.

I DEMAND AN APOLOGY!

TAKEN FROM ACTS 16

GETTING READY

Spend a few moments in prayer talking to God. Ask Him to examine your life and help you to take your eyes off your own problems and place them back on Him.

THE JOURNEY

Have you ever been unfairly blamed for something you didn't do? How did you respond?

"Go where?!" Silas and Timothy asked as they looked at Paul in disbelief.

"Macedonia," Paul confidently answered. "I had a vision of a man standing and calling out, 'Come over to Macedonia and help us'," Paul replied. "I believe God wants us to go there."

Since Barnabas and Paul had split company, there were now two missionary teams. Barnabas had taken Mark and gone back to Cyprus. Paul and Silas had returned to Derbe and Lystra (where Paul had been stoned on his first missionary trip!). While there, Paul met a young believer named Timothy who was strong in his faith. Needing help, Paul

had invited Timothy to join them while he and Silas delivered the
Jerusalem Council decisions to the rapidly growing Gentile churches.

"Macedonia," Paul repeated, and soon the three were sailing for a
place farther west than they had ever been before. After many days, they
finally arrived at the Roman colony and military outpost of Philippi
which was on the Roman highway. Philippi was the leading city in the
region of Macedonia, and Philippi's citizens had rights as Romans. The
people were treated as if they actually lived in Italy.

There was no synagogue so Paul and his companions went outside
the city gate and down to the river where they expected to find a place of
prayer. As they rounded the corner and cleared the bushes, Paul noticed a
group of women who had gathered to pray on the Sabbath. One of them
was a very wealthy woman named Lydia. Lydia made fine, purple fabric.
As Paul preached God's Word to the women, Lydia's heart was opened
and she and her whole household believed and were baptized!

One day as Paul and his companions walked down to the river, they
met a slave girl controlled by an evil spirit. The slave girl had an unusual
demon-empowered ability to predict people's futures. While she did this,
her owners gleefully pocketed all the money earned from the results of
her abilities. For many days the slave girl followed Paul around loudly
proclaiming, "These men who tell you how to be saved are servants of the
Most High God."

Even though this was a true statement, Paul would not accept testimony from demons. He turned to the slave girl and in the power of
Jesus' name commanded the evil spirit to come out of her. Immediately,
the demon left, along with the girl's ability to predict the future.

The owners were furious! Their source of earning easy money was
gone. With clenched teeth and hissing threats, they grabbed Paul and the
others and dragged them before the authorities. "These Jewish men are
causing great trouble in our city!" they accused. "They are pushing customs that are unlawful for us Romans to accept or practice!" they lied.
They had to think up something that would be punishable, for they
wanted to get even with Paul and Silas.

Not given a chance to defend themselves, Paul and Silas were severely flogged and thrown into a prison cell with their feet fastened in stocks. Orders were given to guard them carefully.

Paul and Silas knew they had done nothing wrong. Instead of becoming bitter or resentful, they prayed and sang songs of praise! Prisoners in nearby cells listened with amazement as songs of praise echoed in the damp darkness. Suddenly, the ground began to shake violently. Fear rippled through the prisoner's minds. Would they be buried alive? The prison shook as the cell doors flew open and chains came loose. When the jailer woke up and saw this, he drew his sword. If his prisoners had escaped, he would be killed in their place. *Better to kill myself now than be executed later,* the jailer thought. "Stop!" Paul shouted as the jailer was ready to lean upon his sword. "We are all here; do not harm yourself!"

The region of Macedonia is part of today's Europe.

The jailer couldn't believe his eyes. He fell trembling before Paul and Silas. "What shall I do to be saved?" he asked humbly.

"Believe on the Lord Jesus Christ, and you will be saved," Paul responded. The jailer did just that.

Washing their wounds and giving them all food to eat, the jailer was filled with joy because he had come to believe in God——he and his whole family!

Even though the order sent from the authorities the next day said, "Release those men," Paul and Silas refused to go.

"No," they replied. "We were beaten publicly without a trial and thrown in prison even though we ourselves are Roman citizens. Are we really expected to leave quietly as if nothing happened? No! Let the authorities come and personally escort us out!" they replied.

When the authorities heard that Paul and Silas were Roman citizens, they were alarmed and came apologizing. Upon being escorted out of the prison, Paul and Silas went to Lydia's home in order to encourage her household before leaving Philippi.

Read Acts 16:36, 37 in your own Bible. Why do you think Paul and Silas did this? Were they getting even? Because they were able to praise God, we know that was not the case. Rather, Paul and Silas knew their receiving of an official apology would help officially protect the other believers in Philippi from being treated in the same manner.

When you are unfairly blamed, do you concentrate on your own problems, or are you concerned about others?

GREAT RESULTS!

TAKEN FROM ACTS 19—20

GETTING READY

Spend some time in prayer, allowing God to examine your heart and life. Ask Him to help you understand the importance of your actions and the effects they have on others. Give Him permission to change the things that need to be changed.

THE JOURNEY

Have you ever noticed how one person's actions influence the actions and attitudes of those around him or her?

Apollos was in Corinth when Paul returned to Ephesus on his third (and what would be final) missionary journey. Entering the synagogue in Ephesus, Paul spoke boldly for three months until the non-believing Jews started causing trouble. Because of their actions, Paul met with the believers in another place where he continued preaching for two years.

During this time, God did wonderful miracles through Paul. Handkerchiefs touched by Paul brought healing to those in need. Demons were cast out and God's Word was boldly proclaimed. Because of Paul's actions, great interest in Jesus spread. Even those who didn't know Jesus used His name to provide extra power. The sons of Sceva tried to cast out a demon using Jesus' name. They did not know Jesus for themselves.

"Jesus I know," the demon replied, "and I know about Paul, but who are you?" As quickly as the demon had spoken, he gave supernatural strength to the demon-possessed man who jumped and attacked the men. Screaming, bleeding, naked, and in fear of their lives, the sons of Sceva ran out of the house. When word about this spread around Ephesus, people treated the Lord's name with greater honor. As a result, many believed and openly confessed their evil deeds. Those who practiced magic and sorcery brought their scrolls to be burned. There was a new importance in knowing and honoring Jesus.

"What!" exclaimed Demetrius, a silversmith who fashioned false gods. "If this Christianity keeps up, it will ruin my business!" Angry and greedy, he started a disturbance against Christianity and Paul. "Men, you know we make good money from our business," he said, speaking to other idol makers. "Paul has said our gods are not gods at all! The people have stopped buying our idols, and have robbed our great goddess Artemis of her place of honor in our city!"

Those who heard this grew furious and soon the whole city was in an uproar. Much like a huge tidal wave, the town rushed into the theater chanting, "Great is Artemis of the Ephesians!" They shouted for two solid hours as the crowd formed into a riot. It wasn't until a city official came and spoke to them that they eventually calmed down and went home.

Paul continued preaching the Word of God wherever he went. He traveled to many places encouraging the believers.

When Paul reached Miletus, he asked the leaders of the churches in Ephesus to join him. He was warned by the Holy Spirit of hardship and prison ahead, and knew this would be his last chance to say farewell: "You observed my actions and know that I was not afraid to speak the truth. My only desire now is to complete the task the Lord has given me—the task of proclaiming His Gospel. After I leave, others will rise up and confuse the truth. Stand firm and be on your guard! I turn you over to God and the power of His Word which builds you up."

The rest of the story: Paul prayed for them, then set sail for Jerusalem. While in Jerusalem, he was captured and left to rot in prison for many years. Upon finally getting a hearing, Paul was sent to Rome to stand trial before Caesar. While enroute to Rome, he survived a shipwreck, only to spend several more years imprisoned in Rome awaiting his trial before Caesar! It was during this imprisonment that Paul wrote the books of Ephesians, Philippians, Colossians, and Philemon. (You can read about Paul's adventures in Acts, chapters 21—28.

CLIMBING ONWARD

Whether we realize it or not, our actions effect those around us either for good or for bad. Look up Acts 19:18-20 in your Bible. What happened as a result of their doing this? (See verse 20.)

Skill Time

Take a quick inventory of your life. How is God using you? (Is He able to use you?) Do your actions point others to Jesus, or do they point people away from Him? Tell God about it. Ask His forgiveness for the things you have recently done which were not honoring to Him.

GETTING YOUR BEARINGS:
THE BOOK OF ROMANS

Paul wrote this letter (which we call the Book of Romans) while he was in Corinth for three months on his third missionary journey. His letter was addressed to all believers, Jews and Gentiles, living in Rome.

Since Paul hadn't been to Rome to share the Gospel, where did these believers come from? Perhaps some were the visitors who had traveled to Jerusalem and had become believers during Pentecost (see Acts 2). Others may have been believers who had traveled to Rome during the twenty-seven years since Pentecost, before Paul's writing of this letter.

Paul's purpose in writing this letter was to provide a detailed explanation of the Gospel message he proclaimed. Hoping to visit Rome after delivering gifts to the Jerusalem church (see Acts 21), he was preparing the believers in Rome for a visit. Paul eventually visited Rome, but not in the way and manner he had intended.

Romans is an exciting book through which to journey! It's much like climbing to the top of a mountain and being able to see everything around you for miles. It provides an understanding of the big picture. As you journey through Romans, learn from the foundation it provides. Take a look around you. Romans clearly shows what you (and all people) are like, and what God has done and desires to do for you.

DID YOU HEAR?

TAKEN FROM ROMANS 1—5

GETTING READY

Before you journey today, make sure your heart is in the right place. Ask God to forgive any bad attitude you might have, so your heart and mind are pure and teachable.

THE JOURNEY

What do you say to the person who asks: "If God is loving, how could He send people to hell?" or "What about the people in Africa who have never heard about Jesus?"

There were many things Paul desired to share with the believers in Rome. The message of the Gospel burned in his heart as he gripped a pen and began writing. "I am not ashamed of the Gospel, because it is God's power of salvation to all who believe," Paul passionately wrote to the Romans. "In the Gospel, a righteousness from God is made known to us. This righteousness cannot come from ourselves, for we all have sinned and fall short of God's glory. We have turned to our own ways. No one can be made righteous by keeping the law because the law merely points out our sin and cannot save us from it."

Paul paused for a moment to collect his thoughts, then continued. "But our righteousness from God comes through faith in Jesus Christ. It is freely offered to all who believe."

Paul also explained the importance of the Gospel message and how all must hear about it— even those who live in the far away places of the world. Because God allowed His invisible qualities and power to be seen through what He created (nature), all men are without excuse. No one can look upon nature without realizing there is a God.

"Instead of acknowledging God as God," Paul wrote, "people began worshipping what God created, and even bowed down to images made by their own hands. Thinking themselves wise, they became fools and God gave them over to their evil desires. As a result of their sinful ways their lives were filled with jealousy, selfishness, anger, pride, lying, greed, and an unbelieving heart. When man was at his worst and powerless to help himself, God showed His love by sending Jesus to bear the punishment and pay the penalty for sin—the penalty for sin is death.

"It is because of Christ's blood," Paul reminded the believers, "that we have the ability to be declared 'not guilty' and escape God's judgment. This is the message of the Gospel of which I am not ashamed to preach. This is the message that everyone must hear."

Why is Christ's blood mentioned so often? Blood is the very thing that carries life in our bodies. When our skin is cut, our bodies bleed. The bleeding is actually cleansing our wound so infection won't set in. It washes away the dirt and also carries the agents for healing. This is what Christ's blood does for us spiritually; it "washes away our sin" and heals our relationship with God so we can stand before Him blameless and holy.

CLIMBING ONWARD

God never *sends* anyone to hell. He desires for all to come to know Him. Because of this, God has shown Himself in simple ways so that all people can have opportunity to know He exists. He has also provided a way for man's sins to be forgiven so they would not have to experience eternal punishment in hell.

Look up Romans 3:22-24 and read it. What, then, about those who have never heard about Jesus? As stated in verse 23, all people stand guilty before God; even those who have never heard about Jesus.

Thought: If God is big enough to provide for people's sin, is He not also big enough to provide an opportunity to hear the Gospel for people wanting to know Him?

Skill Time

Everyone is under God's judgment, regardless of what they have and have not heard. Paul brings up an urgent matter in Romans 10:14, 15. Turn there in your Bible and read it. Are you willing to be used by God to help others hear the Gospel? If you are, tell that to God right now. Tell Him you are one who is willing to be "sent" to tell others. Mark this verse in your Bible and put today's date next to it. Refer to it often as a reminder of the commitment you made.

I GIVE UP

TAKEN FROM ROMANS 6—8

GETTING READY

Stop and spend some time talking with God. Don't be afraid to admit your shortcomings to Him. He already knows about them anyway. Thank Him for His love, power, and strength that are available to you.

THE JOURNEY

Has living the Christian life ever seemed impossible to you?

"What I want to do I don't do, and the evil I don't want to do I end up doing!" Paul wrote to the Romans. He didn't write to complain, but rather to comfort them. Even though God had done great things in and through his life, Paul still struggled with sin. "I find this law at work: when I want to do good, evil is right there with me. My heart desires to do God's will, but my mind and my body are waging war against me, creating great difficulties."

Beads of sweat dripped down Paul's face and onto the parchment. Paul wrote from his heart as God directed his words. "What a wretched man I am! Who will rescue me from this body of death? Thanks be to God—through Jesus Christ our Lord!"

The words flowed from the tip of Paul's pen as he continued to write, explaining how Christ sets people free from being helpless slaves to sin. "For sin is no longer our master. We have been set free from it and are no longer under its all-controlling power."

Faith is an everyday thing, not just a salvation thing. It is believing in God's character rather than our own. F-A-I-T-H; Forsaking-All-I-Trust-Him.

Paul paused a moment and thought about his own life—his victories and his struggles. He gripped his pen and passionately wrote from his heart. "Yet, we must still wrestle with our sinful nature (natural desires toward sin), but we don't have to be defeated! The Holy Spirit gives us the help and strength we need to overcome sinful desires in our lives. Even when our struggles are so great that we don't know how to pray for ourselves, the Holy Spirit prays for us in ways that words cannot express. Things impossible for us become possible with God. As we depend upon the Holy Spirit, He will help us live in a way that shows our love to God and honors Him. There will be difficult times, but we must never forget that God works all things together for our good. He is in control. If our God is for us, then who can be against us? There is nothing that can separate us from the love of God. Because of what Christ Jesus did for us, we stand as more than conquerors in Him."

"I am convinced," Paul wrote with joy, "that neither death nor life, neither angels nor demons, nor anything else will be able to separate us from the love of God that is in Christ Jesus our Lord."

Find Romans 8:8 in your Bible and read it. Now, skip down to verse 14 and compare. By whom should we be led?

DANGER AHEAD

As you walk with God there will be times when you forget to depend on His strength and try to live the Christian life on your own. Don't! You will only become defeated and unable to live a life honoring and pleasing to God. Instead, ask God for His strength.

It's Not My Problem!

TAKEN FROM ROMANS 14—15

Getting Ready

Stop and pray. Ask God to show you areas in your life that might be affecting others in a negative way, turning them *from* the Lord rather than *to* Him.

The Journey

W hy do you think some kids act big and brag about what they are allowed to do?

Paul picked up his pen and continued writing to the believers in Rome. There was so much to tell them! They had been enjoying great freedom in Christ; yet with that freedom came responsibility. Some believers who were weak in their faith still desired to hold tightly to the Law. As they did so, they were tempted to think of themselves as more religious than others.

Those who were stronger in their faith enjoyed their freedom in Christ without thinking about how it might affect those who were weaker. The stronger Christians knew that meat in itself was not evil. It was merely food—even meat that had once been offered to idols. Nothing in Scripture forbade them to eat of it. The younger believers, however, had great difficulty with this idea. They not only refused to eat it themselves, but they also struggled in their hearts with those who did. Perhaps without knowing it, the stronger Christians were causing the weaker Christians to struggle in their faith.

"Even if what you're doing is not wrong," Paul wrote, "but it causes others to have difficulties, it then becomes something wrong. Don't judge or blame one another, but determine in your heart to build each other up. You who are stronger believers should be willing to stop doing something that causes weaker believers to stumble in their faith—even if what you are doing is not wrong."

Paul paused a moment, then continued. The words flowed off his pen and onto the parchment as the Holy Spirit continued to guide Paul in his writing. "Do not destroy God's working in another person's life for the sake of doing something God might allow you to do. It would be far better not to do that thing than to do it and cause a roadblock in someone else's faith."

Paul called some believers "weaker brothers" for they still wanted to earn God's favor through the keeping of Jewish laws and traditions.

CLIMBING ONWARD

Check out Romans 14:12, 13. To whom do we have to answer to? What two things are we not to do to our fellow brothers and sisters in Christ? Skip down to verse 19 and read that. (Go on! It's a great verse.) *Edification* means "to build up or strengthen another."

THINKING on your FEET

When you have opportunity to do something that God allows you to enjoy (but you know it might cause a fellow believer to struggle in his faith), what will you do?

GETTING YOUR BEARINGS:
THE BOOK OF I CORINTHIANS

First Corinthians is a letter Paul wrote to the struggling church in Corinth. It was written while he stayed in Ephesus for two and a half years while on his third missionary journey (see Acts 19).

Corinth at that time was one of the greatest trading and commercial centers in the world. It was located on an isthmus (a narrow strip of land joining two larger bodies of land) that was four miles across. In order for people to travel from the northern part of Greece to the southern part, they had to pass through Corinth. Because it was dangerous to sail around the southern tip of Greece, sailors often dragged their ships out of the water at Corinth, put them on rollers and hauled them across the isthmus. If the boat was too big to be rolled across, the cargo was unloaded and carried across the isthmus (through Corinth) and placed on ships waiting at the other side.

Because of all this activity, Corinth became famous for its trading and markets. Luxuries came into the city from every land imaginable. People living in Corinth became known for their love of drunkenness and evil abounded. Temples for idol worship were many.

In the midst of all this evil, Corinth had a church that was struggling with its own set of problems. Paul received word about those problems and wrote I Corinthians in answer to them.

As you journey through I Corinthians, look about you and take note of their problems. Do you see some of the same ones we face today?

"Oh Yeah? Well I . . ."

TAKEN FROM I CORINTHIANS 1—3

Getting Ready

As you prepare to journey today, ask God to examine your thoughts, actions, and attitudes. Ask Him to change what needs to be changed so you can live a life honoring to Him. Thank Him for the help He gives through His Holy Spirit.

The Journey

Do your friends ever brag about how great they are because of the church they go to? How does this make you feel?

"Oh yeah?! Well I follow Paul's teaching."
"That's nothing. I follow Apollos; he's really good."
"No way! Cephas is the best."
"Oh yeah! Well I follow Christ! So there!"

Arguments like these arose in the church at Corinth. Those who claimed to follow Paul were probably Gentile believers who had heard the Gospel through him. Apollos was from Alexandria and was a very intelligent man. Those who claimed loyalty to him were the intellectuals who thought they had more information than others. Jewish believers stood behind Peter (called Cephas), since he had brought the Gospel to the Jews. Those who wanted to outdo the others proudly said they followed Christ. No one could argue with that! There was only one fault with this last group: they weren't saying they belonged to Jesus, but that Jesus belonged to them—and them alone! All of this arguing back and forth was ripping the church apart. It needed to be stopped immediately.

"Do you not realize," Paul wrote, "that Apollos, Peter, and I are nothing? I may have planted the seed of the Gospel, and Apollos may have watered it by the information you got from him, but it is God who has caused the growth. God and God alone is the One who is to receive glory."

Paul continued. "Remember what you were like before you came to know Christ. None of you were overly wise, of royal birth, or the most important people in society. Why do you think of yourselves that way now? Do you not realize that God chooses the weak things of the world to shame the strong? God does this so no one can boast before Him. Let those who boast, boast in the Lord," Paul challenged.

Paul's pen may have tapped the table a few times as he searched for words. "When I came to you, I did not come with wise and persuasive words. I came preaching the simple message of the cross of Christ. I did not come with human wisdom (lest the cross of Christ be emptied of its power), but I came relying on the Spirit's power so that your faith wouldn't rest on man's wisdom, but on God.

"But your focus has come off Christ and onto yourselves. As a result, you quarrel with one another. You are being controlled by your sinful nature rather than by God's Holy Spirit, and God is not honored. When I came to you, I laid down a solid foundation built upon Christ. This, each of you have. Therefore, let each man be careful as to how he builds upon this foundation. Stop boasting about men and start boasting about God, for the thoughts of even the wisest person are foolishness to God."

CLIMBING ONWARD

Read I Corinthians 3:11. A foundation is the most important part of a building and gives the building its value (for without a solid foundation, the building would crumble).

Jesus is a true foundation. Go back a few verses and read I Corinthians 2:5. What is the result of such a foundation? This verse really puts things into perspective!

CROSS ROADS

When you are tempted to brag, will you brag about your church, or will you brag about your God? What foundation are you building upon?

It's My Business

TAKEN FROM I CORINTHIANS 5—6

Getting Ready

Don't rush through this Getting Ready section. Use this time to prepare your heart. It is a time where you get quiet before God and allow Him to speak to you.

The Journey

Have you ever heard someone say, "Leave me alone. What I do is my own business and none of your concern!"

Paul sat back in his chair. Although he had just written about one problem to the church of Corinth, he knew there were other problems he needed to answer before sending his letter. He bent his head and continued to write.

"It has been reported that there is a person among you who is practicing an immoral act. Yet, you proudly stand by and allow him to do it, boasting about the love you are showing him. You should be filled with grief and put him out of your fellowship that he might be alone with his sin and come to realize the damage it causes. Your boasting is not good. Just as it only takes a little bit of yeast to affect a whole batch of dough, it takes only one believer living in sin to affect and hurt fellow believers. Do not associate with those who call themselves believers yet continue sin. The loving thing to do is to put them out so they will realize their sin and turn from it. Don't be afraid to act as a judge in these matters."

Paul set his pen down and rubbed his head. How could he communicate the importance of living a God-honoring life that stands as an example for others to follow? He knew the Corinthian believers were taking each other to court with their complaints and arguments against one another. They were demanding their rights rather than working things out. Paul wrote, "I say this to your shame. One brother is going to court against another—and this is being done in front of unbelievers!"

> Yeast is a substance that, once placed into dough, grows, spreads, and multiplies. You can see yeast working when bread rises or is being baked.

Paul reminded them of the evil they had been rescued from through Jesus Christ. "Slanderers, idol worshippers, thieves, drunkards, immoral people . . . that is what you were. But now your sins are washed away. Through Jesus you have been made holy before God and stand blameless before Him. This was not free or cheap—you were bought with a price, which cost Jesus His life. Therefore, be careful how you live. Each person must choose to honor God with his body and actions, for what you do has an effect on others."

CLIMBING ONWARD

Turn to I Corinthians 6:19, 20 in your Bible. When we become a Christian, God gives His Holy Spirit to live in us. How does God view our bodies? What should we be doing as a result? A good way to help yourself make God-honoring choices is to ask yourself this question before acting: "If Jesus were standing here, what would He say? What would He do?"

CROSS ROADS

Before taking action, do you ask yourself, "What would Jesus do?" or does Jesus have to ask you, "What are you doing?"

No Problem!

TAKEN FROM I CORINTHIANS 10

GETTING READY

Pray, asking God to teach you from His Word. Thank Him that His strength and help are always available to you.

THE JOURNEY

When you are tempted to do bad things, do you ever give in and do them, thinking you can always ask God to forgive you later?

"As I mentioned before," Paul wrote to the Corinthian believers, "don't think just because you are forgiven in Christ you can have freedom to sin. The freedom you have is freedom from the mastery of sin!"

Paul knew the believers in Corinth were tempted to sin and live solely for pleasure. They had reasoned that if their sins were forgiven, no harm could come from adding a few more sins to the list. Because they mistakenly thought this way, they became confident and self-seeking. Their eyes were off of the Lord and on themselves. "Live and be happy" became their motto as they gave into temptations. It was as if they had completely forgotten about God's presence in their lives.

174

The pen moved slowly across the parchment as Paul's thoughts traveled back in time to God's chosen people. He thought about all they had done against God in spite of God's presence with them. "I do not want you to be uninformed," Paul wrote. "The people of Israel under Moses' leadership knew they were God's people (just as you now are), yet God was not pleased with them. They continuously sinned by loving other things more than they loved God. They served idols and put God's love to the test. Wanting to satisfy their own pleasures, they gave in to temptations and grumbled against the leadership God placed over them. As a result, God was forced to punish and discipline them to bring their hearts back to Himself. What happened to the people of Israel stands as an example and a warning to us."

Paul continued, "Know that the temptations you face are common to all men. You don't have to be mastered by them, for in the face of temptation, God remains faithful to you. He will not allow you to be tempted beyond what you can withstand, but offers to you His strength and help. When you are tempted, God provides a way of escape for you. So, whatever you do in word or actions, you have the ability to do it all for the glory of God."

For more information on how Israel gave in to temptation, we can turn to the pages of the Old Testament. The book Exodus is loaded with great background information and gives a close-up look at God's chosen people—faults and all!

CLIMBING ONWARD

Turn to I Corinthians 10:13. (Go ahead, you will need this verse for Skill Time as well.) What does it say? Read it again, emphasizing the words *no, God,* and *but*. What two things does God promise to do for you?

Skill Time

Write I Corinthians 10:13 on an index card and memorize it. Keep the card handy to review the verse as needed. It is a promise you'll need to remember and rely on the rest of your life.

I LOVE YOU, ANYWAY

TAKEN FROM I CORINTHIANS 12—13

GETTING READY

Spend a few moments alone with God. Thank Him that He loves you with a love beyond imagining and that He has given you a special place in the family of believers.

THE JOURNEY

How does it make you feel when kids say you're a nobody and that they're more important than you?

"Nobody is a nobody in God's kingdom," Paul wrote to the Corinthian believers. He was aware of the temptation by some in the church to look down on others. It seemed they were comparing their God-given spiritual gifts and rating them in order of importance.

"Do you not understand?" Paul wrote. "It is the same Holy Spirit who lives in each of you. He doesn't give gifts so you can build yourselves up, but rather to build others up and have the ability to do God's work in God's way," Paul stated. Next Paul listed some of the gifts with which the Holy Spirit empowers believers.

"Each person has a special place in the family of believers, and each person is given special abilities. We are like a body working together. The eye cannot say to the hand, 'I don't need you,' or the foot say to the ear, 'because you are not a foot like me, you are not a part of the body!' No! If all parts were an eye, then how could the body hear? If all were an ear, then how could the body see? All parts of the body are equally important. We are the body of Christ, and each of us has been given different abilities," Paul stated.

"Therefore, don't seek certain gifts, thinking they will make you more important. That kind of thinking is sinful and selfish. Instead, desire to live a life showing God's love. For, if I had the gift of speaking in tongues but didn't have love, I would only be like a noisy clanging cymbal. Even if I could do the greatest and most wonderful things for the glory of God, but didn't have His kind of love in my heart, it would be as if my life counted for nothing. God's kind of love changes lives. It is a love that is patient and kind. People who have God's kind of love in their heart are people who do not envy others, boast, or act in a proud way. They are not rude and do not want the best for themselves. They are not easily angered and don't keep a list of wrongs that have been done against them. God's kind of love enables people to rejoice in the truth, rather than delighting in evil. It always protects, always trusts, always hopes, and always hangs in there no matter what. God's type of love never fails."

Paul continued writing, "Although God has given gifts, they will all pass away—they are only temporary. But God's love will remain forever. Those who have learned to love with God's kind of love are those who desire the greatest thing of all. Faith, hope, and love are what matters, but the greatest of all is love."

Turn to I Corinthians 13:4, 5. In these two verses alone, Paul lists nine descriptions of real love. If these descriptions were rules on how to love (which they are), which of these would the Corinthian believers be guilty of breaking?

Skill Time

Find an index card or piece of paper and number it one through nine. Using your Bible, write down these nine rules on how to love. When you have finished, place a small x by the one(s) that are personally hardest for you. (Remember, loving others with God's type of love is something we can do only by relying on God's strength and help.)

Next, get on your knees and tell God your areas of struggle. Ask Him to forgive you and to provide the strength to love with His kind of love. For the rest of this week, find practical things to do that fit under the areas you marked. Then, with God's help, do them.

GETTING YOUR BEARINGS:
THE BOOK OF II CORINTHIANS

Second Corinthians can almost be viewed as "part two" of a letter written to the church in Corinth. Although the church had corrected one of the problems Paul wrote about in I Corinthians, other problems were quickly developing. Some who were trying to cause trouble in the church began attacking Paul's character. As a result, Paul wrote to defend himself—not for his own sake, but for their's. He knew if they questioned him, they would also question God's message of the Gospel that he proclaimed.

While journeying through II Corinthians, remember it was written while Paul was on his third missionary journey. Because of a riot by the silversmiths in Ephesus (see Acts 19), Paul found himself in the region of Macedonia where he met up with Titus and received news of the church in Corinth. The general well-being of the church was good, although there was bad news about a group in the church rising up against Paul.

As you journey through this book, notice Paul's love for the church even though it caused him great pain. Notice how he handled some of the problems and encouraged them to remain true to the Lord by living in a way that is honoring to God. Think about your own life and how it measures up.

READ MY LIFE

TAKEN FROM II CORINTHIANS 2—5

GETTING READY

Take a few minutes to tell God the struggles you have with others. Open your heart, for He has a listening ear. Now, ask Him to point out any areas in your life that make other people struggle. Don't be afraid, for God loves you with a perfect love, and He will never give up on you.

THE JOURNEY

Do you sometimes have a hard time getting along with other Christians? Since we all serve the same God, why do we disagree and argue?

Paul's letter contained some harsh words to the Corinthian believers. It seemed the problems were getting worse! Since Paul's first letter, more trouble had occurred and the church became torn with other difficulties. Having obeyed Paul's instruction about disciplining the believer living in sin, they were now unwilling to forgive him! Even though he had turned from his sin and had asked forgiveness, some in the church insisted on even harsher punishment. A great argument arose that caused disunity and bitterness.

"The punishment first given was enough and all that is needed," Paul wrote, "for it was successful in turning the person away from his sin. Now, however, you should forgive and comfort him. Welcome him back and don't hold a grudge against him, for this only causes division among you that results in bitterness and an opportunity for Satan to gain a victory."

Paul went on to explain how the believers' lives were like a letter that people could read. They were not to be individual letters, but one, working together in unity to communicate one message—and that to the glory of God. Their ability to love and forgive one another would carry a strong message to the world—a message that couldn't be easily ignored.

In John 13:35, Jesus said: "By this all men will know you are my disciples—if you have love for one another."

Paul knew it didn't take much to look at their failures and become discouraged. Even though the church had great difficulties, they still belonged to God, and God had greater things for them.

"Our goodness and our abilities don't come from ourselves, but from God," Paul reminded, "and God chooses to carry His message in us much like we use jars of clay to carry treasures. Through Jesus, God brought us to Himself and He desires to use us to carry this same Good News and hope to others. Therefore, fix your eyes on that which you cannot see— those things which are eternal, not the problems you have with one another. Make it your goal to live a life pleasing to God, and forgive the one who has turned from his sin. Whatever you do, do not forget that all believers will stand before Jesus and be judged according to what they have done—both good and bad."

CLIMBING ONWARD

Look up II Corinthians 3:18. What do we reflect? Who's likeness should we find ourselves being changed into? Is this something we can do on our own, or take credit for? Why?

DANGER AHEAD

Our life is like a letter that others read, and yet in and of our own strength, we are like frail clay pots! There will be times in your life that you have a difficult time forgiving or loving a brother or sister in Christ. Instead of focusing on your own feelings, think about what your actions and life might be saying to those who are watching. Turn it over to God and ask Him to change your heart so you can do what God would have you to do.

Oops!

TAKEN FROM II CORINTHIANS 8—9

GETTING READY

Stop and pray. Thank the Lord for His work in your life—even in the smallest of details. Ask Him to continue to help you live a life honoring to Him.

THE JOURNEY

Have you ever promised to give money to something and failed to follow through? What happened?

Paul continued writing to the believers in Corinth while he stayed in a region called Macedonia. In Macedonia, there were three churches Paul had started—one in Philippi, one in Thessalonica, and one in Berea. The believers in these churches knew Paul was collecting an offering for the needy church in Jerusalem and they had promised to give generously without being asked. . . .

Paul tapped the pen on the parchment and searched for the right words. There were many problems in the church at Corinth, but the church had eagerly desired to show their love and concern for the poor in Jerusalem. As a matter of fact, they were the first ones to respond with a promise and desire to give. Now, a year had gone by and they had not followed through on their promise. Paul knew they needed to be encouraged.

"Brothers, I want you to know about the grace that God gave to the Macedonian churches," Paul wrote, holding them up as an example. "For even though they themselves were poor and suffering, they gave as much as they were able—and even beyond their ability! On their own, they pleaded with us to share in this ministry of giving to the needy church of Jerusalem. They did not do as we expected, but beyond. Because of their example, we have urged Titus to come so you might have the opportunity to give that which you promised earlier," he wrote.

"Please understand that I am not commanding you to give, but rather encouraging you to show the trueness of your love. I know since last year you were ready to give. I boasted about it to the Macedonians, telling them of your eagerness to help. As a result of your example, many of them desired to give to the cause too. Titus and some brothers are now being sent in order that our boasting about you should not prove empty, but that you might be ready and able to give as I said you would be. When they arrive, do not have a bad attitude and give because you feel you have to or because everyone else is giving. Let each person give as he has decided in his heart to give, for God loves someone who gives willingly. As you give, you not only will be helping the needs of God's people, but also your generosity will result in thanksgiving to God. The hearts of those who receive your gift will be with you because of the work of God's grace in your lives."

A tithe is an Old Testament rule of thumb that involves regularly giving 10 percent of what you earn. An offering is anything given above and beyond the tithe as an act of worship, determined by the giver's heart.

Find II Corinthians 9:7, 8 and read it.. Read it a second time. According to these verses, what does God promise to do for us?

Skill Time

Think over the things you have promised to give to but never did. Perhaps it was a portion of your allowance for a Sunday school project or the support of a missionary or needy child. If at all possible, try to make it right and pay what you promised. Know that God will be honored and you will be more blessed than those who receive your gift!

AND HERE'S THE PROOF

TAKEN FROM II CORINTHIANS 10—13

GETTING READY

Before you journey today, ask the Holy Spirit to teach you and help you to understand God's Word. Thank the Lord for His faithfulness and power to help you change what needs to be changed in your life.

THE JOURNEY

Do you know people who think better of themselves than they should?

Paul's hand was steady and sure as the words poured from his pen. These were the last thoughts in his letter to the Corinthians, and he had saved the most difficult issue for last.

Ever since Titus had given Paul the report of a group rising up against him in the church, the news burned in his heart. The men opposing him were false apostles who accused Paul without cause. He knew these false apostles were only trying to gain things for themselves and really had no love for the church. Paul knew they carried a different gospel, which was no gospel at all. Because of this, Paul was forced to speak up and put the matter to rest—not for his own sake, but for the sake of the Corinthian believers.

As much as Paul didn't like talking about himself, he pushed the pen to the parchment and continued to write. The false apostles had accused Paul of being bold in his letters, but cowardly in person. Paul was also accused of being wrong for not living from the hand of what the Corinthian believers provided. In addition, he was accused of possibly dipping into the money collections for the church in Jerusalem!

"What we are in our letters, we will be in our actions. For we destroy arguments and ideas that set themselves up against the knowledge of God," Paul wrote. He thought about how the false apostles were taking advantage of those in the church. "As for not accepting your support of my ministry, you know that I did not want to become a burden to you. Why should I rob from the poor? Let it be known that I came only to give, not to take for myself— which is something those who speak against me do," Paul answered. He knew the false apostles boasted about themselves and their pretend accomplishments. They even carried special papers telling others how great they were. "They come to you boasting about themselves—but I come to you boasting about Christ. Let him who boasts, boast in the Lord."

Carrying letters of approval was a common practice in the first century. Paul, however, said his approval came from God.

Paul continued on, describing how the false apostles were taking credit for work done by God through him, and how they made themselves look official and important. "They boast in the ways of the world," Paul said. "Just for this moment, I too will boast in this way so you may fully see and understand.

"Are they Hebrews? So am I. Are they Abraham's descendants? So am I. Are they servants of Christ? I am more. I have worked much harder, been in prison more often, been beaten more severely, and been exposed to death over and over. Five times I was beaten from the Jews with thirty-nine lashes. Three times I was beaten with rods, once I was stoned, three times I was shipwrecked, I spent a day and a night in the open sea, and I have been always on the move. I have been in danger from rivers, bandits, my own countrymen, and Gentiles. I have been in danger in the country, in the city, at sea, and from false brothers. I have worked hard and have often gone without sleep and food. I have known hunger and thirst and have been cold and naked. Besides all this, and if this isn't enough, my heart remains greatly concerned for all the churches.

It has been thought that Paul's "thorn in the flesh" was fading eyesight, or even severe headaches.

"Even if I could have boasted about these things to you, I did not do so in the past, for I did not want anyone to think more of me than they should. Also, to keep me from becoming prideful, God gave me a weakness like a thorn in my flesh that forces me to have to depend upon Him. Therefore, I will gladly boast about my weakness, for it is through my weakness that Christ's power is made perfect in me, for when I am weak, then I am strong."

Paul continued, "The reason I write all this is not to defend myself, but to strengthen you. And these things about me you already know. Don't be taken in by false apostles, nor listen to a gospel other than what I preached to you. Examine yourselves; test yourselves to see if you are really in the faith."

Look up II Corinthians 13:5 in your own Bible. What does it say? A good way to test yourself is to check your motives for doing and saying things. Why do you do what you do?

If you were put on trial and had to give an account of yourself, would you need to say anything, or would the sincerity of your life and actions speak for themselves?

GETTING YOUR BEARINGS:
THE BOOK OF GALATIANS

The book of Galatians is a letter Paul wrote to the believers in the Gentile region of Galatia. These churches began as a result of Paul's first missionary journey (Acts 13—14) when he visited the cities of Pisidian-Antioch, Iconium, Lystra, and Derbe. As you may remember, these cities held great adventure and trials for Paul as he faithfully preached the Gospel before being run out of town or stoned.

Paul wrote this letter to the Galatians from his home church in Antioch just before the meeting of the council of Jerusalem. He had just received word that some were trying to force their Jewish rules upon the new believers. Paul wrote to remind the believers of how they had come to Christ.*

Galatians is a strong and foundational book, much like the book of Romans. It has sometimes been called a short Romans because it is packed with important facts of our faith called doctrine. One such doctrine is the fact that no one can earn their way into heaven by trying to keep God's rules. Salvation from the penalty and power of sin comes only through God's grace—not our own efforts.

As you journey through Galatians, keep your eyes open and see how many other faith facts you discover.

*NOTE: This book was written before the book of Romans and Corinthians, even though in our Bibles it comes after them. Don't let this confuse you! The New Testament is not put together in the order it was written. That is why it is important to GET YOUR BEARINGS before you journey through a book of the Bible. Knowing the background first will help you better understand what you are reading.

NICE WORK

TAKEN FROM GALATIANS 1—3

GETTING READY

Pray, asking the Lord to give you a teachable heart so you can learn and grow even closer to Him. Thank Him for what He has done for you through Jesus Christ.

THE JOURNEY

Do you know people who are following the rules, trying to impress everybody—including God?

Paul's anger burned just thinking about it. A group of Jews were going around the churches in Galatia trying to convert the believers to Judaism. "You must first become Jews in order to have salvation," the group called "Judaizers" said. "Then you must dedicate your life to carrying out all the rules of the law, for that is how you can win God's favor," they proclaimed. The Judaizers believed that only Jews were given the special privilege of salvation. They proclaimed a false gospel by telling people to depend on the laws of Moses for salvation. They even went a step further and accused Paul of making religion easy in order to win the favor of men! It was to these issues that Paul quickly wrote to the churches in Galatia who were being taken in by this false teaching.

"I am shocked that you are turning from God who called you by the grace of Christ, and turning to a different gospel which is really no gospel at all! If anyone is preaching anything different to you than what you heard from me, let him be condemned! Even if I myself came, or an angel with a different message, don't listen! For the Gospel I gave you is not something made up by man; it is from God," Paul wrote.

"What people say about me makes no difference, for my Master is God." Paul defended himself. "If I were trying to win the approval of men, as the Judaizers accuse, I would not be a servant of Christ. Let it be known that I bear the marks of being His servant on my body. The life I live in my body, I now live by faith in Jesus who loved me and gave Himself for me."

Paul sat back and thought about the possible results of the Judaizers' false message. He knew it was turning hearts from a faith in Christ to a false religious faith—one where man felt he could become good enough to impress God and earn his way into heaven.

"That's wrong!" Paul screamed in his heart as he picked up the pen and started writing. "It is only through faith in Jesus and His works of righteousness that we can be holy enough to stand before God! God gave His laws to show us His standards of righteousness. These laws cannot deliver us from our sin, for they were given to point out our sins. If we could become righteous by keeping God's law, then Jesus died for nothing."

Paul challenged, "Oh friends, are you so foolish? Did God give you His Spirit and work miracles among you because you were perfect, or because you believed in Him? After beginning with the Spirit, do you now insult God by going back to thinking you can impress Him with your own works of righteousness?

CLIMBING ONWARD

Look up Galatians 3:1. What do the first few words say? (HINT: It is an exclamation Paul makes about the Galatians.) Now, skip down to verse 3. What does Paul say they are doing?

DANGER AHEAD

There are people who say you can't please God unless you keep a certain number of religious rules—or at least the rules they live by! Don't believe them. Live for Christ and your life will automatically be honoring and pleasing to God.

FRUIT, ANYONE?

TAKEN FROM GALATIANS 5

GETTING READY

As you prepare your heart, ask God to quiet your thoughts and keep you from being distracted. Ask Him to honor your time with Him and teach you through His Holy Spirit.

THE JOURNEY

What do you do in a situation where there are no rules or people to tell you what is right?

Paul had already told the Galatians it was not necessary to live by the law in order to impress God. Their righteousness came through faith in Christ alone. Since the law was no longer their master and they were no longer slaves to it, did it mean they now had the freedom to do wrong?

"It was for freedom that Jesus Christ set us free," Paul wrote. "This freedom is a freedom *from* sin, not a freedom *to* sin! Therefore, don't use your freedom to do whatever you want, but use it to do what is right by serving one another in love."

Paul continued, "If you live by the Spirit you will not do what the sinful nature desires—acts such as: doing things that make you unfit to come before God; desiring pleasure so much that you don't care what others say or think; loving something more than you love God; witch-craft; hatred; arguing; desiring to have what others have; losing your temper; looking out only for yourself; not getting along with others; and living for your own enjoyment. Those who live by the desires of the sinful nature will never enter the kingdom of God."

> Sinful nature is the way we are naturally, without God's help. Sometimes Paul refers to it as "the flesh." Paul is not talking about skin, but rather something that is common to all mankind—the desire toward sin.

Paul thought a minute and then wrote, "Those who belong to Jesus don't live by the sinful nature and its desires; they live by the Spirit. The fruit of the Spirit is much different than the acts of the flesh. The fruit of the Spirit seeks nothing but the best for others (even if others seek only the worst for you); has a confidence and peace in difficult times; accepts others (faults and all); shows kind-ness and allows God's goodness to shine; trusts God; is teachable (not proud); respects others; and does not give in to temptations and sinful desires. Since we have new life by the Spirit, let us walk by the Spirit's power, and not by the power of our sinful nature."

CLIMBING ONWARD

Find Galatians 5:16 and read it. How can we keep from doing the wrong thing—even when there seem to be no rules? Skip down to verses 22-23. What are the results of doing this?

Skill Time

Look back at verse 22. Notice that it says the fruit of the Spirit, not the fruits! It is not a shopping list from which to pick and choose! A good test to see if you are walking in the Holy Spirit's power is to copy the list down, review it often, and measure your life by it.

If you fail in one area, you can be sure you are not living a Spirit-filled life. When you see this happening, talk to God. Tell Him what you have done wrong and ask for His forgiveness. Ask to be controlled by His Holy Spirit rather than your own sinful nature. God is faithful and will answer your prayers—even when you fail over and over and have to keep coming to Him with this prayer! For the next five days, practice doing this and see the difference it makes in your life.

COUNT ME OUT

TAKEN FROM GALATIANS 6

GETTING READY

Before you finish journeying through Galatians today, take a moment to thank God for the Holy Spirit who lives in you (if you have trusted Jesus as your Savior), and for the way He helps you to live a life pleasing to God.

THE JOURNEY

How do you feel when others get away with things they shouldn't?

"Friends," Paul wrote to the believers in Galatia, "if a believer accidently slips and falls into sin (we all make mistakes), those of you who know how to rely on the Holy Spirit should help that believer get back on the right track again. This help needs to be in a gentle and loving way, not with a prideful spirit or one of harsh punishment. As you help your brother, think about yourself so you don't become tempted as well. The one who thinks he can't be tempted is only fooling himself."

Paul thought for a moment then continued his warning. "Each person should compare his own actions to God's standards. Those who compare themselves to others become taken in with a prideful attitude and begin thinking better of themselves than they really ought.

"Do not be deceived: God cannot be mocked. Those who get away with things they shouldn't don't get away with them forever. What a person sows, he will reap the results of later," Paul wrote thinking about the nearby farmers. A particular seed is planted and, even though it doesn't look like anything is happening, the seed begins to grow underground. Roots are sent down and outward to give nourishment to a plant that will soon grow. Not long after that, a tender shoot comes up and a plant begins to grow. Anyone looking at the plant can tell what kind of seed the farmer has planted.

"So it is with your life," Paul compared. "Whoever sows to the sinful nature will reap what the sinful nature has to offer—destruction. But, whoever sows to the Spirit will reap eternal life. Therefore, don't compare yourselves to others in case you become proud. And don't lose heart in doing good," Paul encouraged. "For just like the farmer who planted seed, you too will reap a harvest in due time if you don't give up."

"To reap" means to experience the results or rewards of something. (Sow a tomato plant, reap tomatoes.) It is a common law of physical nature around us (ask any gardener), as well as a common law of human nature (ask God).

CLIMBING ONWARD

Look up Galatians 6:9. This applies to each of us personally—especially when we compare ourselves to others or begin to lose heart. What does it tell us to do? What is the reward?

DANGER AHEAD

In your lifetime you will see people doing wrong things and seeming to get away with it! Don't become discouraged, deceived, or decide to live like them. Sooner or later they will pay the penalty for their actions. Instead, keep your eyes and your focus on Christ; that is what matters most.

GETTING YOUR BEARINGS:
THE BOOK OF EPHESIANS

Ephesians was written while Paul was a prisoner in Rome after his third missionary journey. Many say this is Paul's greatest writing and is much different than his other writings. Perhaps a reason for this is that Paul was not writing to correct any problems in a church. Being a prisoner, he had plenty of time to write a letter about the things on his heart—a letter not only to the church at Ephesus, but one to be shared with other churches in the neighboring areas as well.

Journeying through Ephesians is much like journeying through a gold mine! Each verse is loaded with great nuggets of truth waiting to be explored! Through Ephesians we are reminded of the spiritual blessings we have in Christ; of how we have the privilege of standing before God in righteousness; of instructions for living; and of instructions for spiritual battle!

As you journey through Ephesians, take your time. If you see a gold nugget that catches your eye, stop, dig it up, and examine it. One way to do this is to ask questions. Then, using a Bible study tool, such as a concordance (usually found in the back of a Bible), look up a word and read the other verses in Scripture where that word is used. If you didn't find an answer to your question, ask your parents, Sunday school teacher, or pastor to help you. Who knows, God could use your question to teach them something too!

WHAT A PICKER-UPPER!

TAKEN FROM EPHESIANS 1

GETTING READY

Before you journey today, ask the Lord to forgive you for not always appreciating what He has done for you. Thank Him for how deeply and completely He loves you.

THE JOURNEY

Do you sometimes feel like a real nobody? Do you ever wish you could be someone else rather than who you are?

Paul wrote to the believers in Ephesus, "May you experience the grace and peace God offers you." He sat back and thought about the wonders of God's love, then picked up his pen and began flooding the parchment with words.

"Praise be to God who has blessed us with every spiritual blessing in Christ! For He chose us—even before the creation of the world—to be holy and blameless in His sight. He planned for us, in love, to be adopted into His heavenly family. He

> In Christ you have been chosen, planned for, adopted, forgiven, guaranteed an inheritance, empowered, loved, and accepted.

freely gave to us His grace through Jesus, and it is in Jesus we have the forgiveness of sins."

Paul's mind recalled God's grace. "God keeps pouring out the riches of His grace upon us in all wisdom and understanding—even today! He allows us to know His will, and He brings everything together under one headship—Christ's. In Jesus we were chosen by God—who works out everything according to His will, and we exist for the praise of His glory! Because we believed in Jesus whom God sent, we were sealed with the Holy Spirit, who is God's guarantee to us that we have an inheritance."

> The worth of something is based on the value experts give it. God made you, and He is the expert of experts! He places a high value on you and stands behind His words with proof and actions!

Paul paused for a moment, then continued to write. "I keep asking God that He may give you wisdom so that you may know Him better. I pray your heart will be opened so you might know the hope to which He has called you, the riches of His inheritance, and His awesome power for us who believe!"

Paul's heart yearned for the believers to know and experience all the blessings God has for them. He knew if they could only understand who they are in Christ, it would keep them from great difficulties, disappointments, and temptations. No longer would they feel unimportant or desire to be like others. No longer would they have the need to compare themselves to others, or strive to win God's favor or approval. They would have all they needed to live a victorious life. If they could only understand who they are in Christ, they would realize they stood complete, totally loved, and accepted in God's sight through Jesus. They could begin to experience a joy that words could never describe! *If only they understood*, Paul thought.

CLIMBING ONWARD

Check out Ephesians 1:18, 19. These are great verses! What three facts can we stand on?

DANGER AHEAD

Your feelings about yourself will come and go—changing several times as you continue to mature. Don't trust them. Feelings are just that: feelings. They are not fact, and they don't usually tell the true story! Don't rely on them. Instead, remember you are God's. If God has thought this highly of you, should you think any less of yourself?

RESCUED!

TAKEN FROM EPHESIANS 2—3

GETTING READY

Stop and pray. Ask God to use His Word to remind you of the most life-changing thing that can ever happen to a person— receiving salvation. Ask Him to keep your heart teachable and excited, no matter how old you may feel.

Have you ever been heroically rescued from something? What happened?

"Lying, cheating, stealing, disobeying, fighting, selfishness, pride, unkindness, being impatient, loving something else more than you love God . . . these are the desires of human nature," Paul wrote.

Perhaps Paul's head was bent as he continued writing to the believers in Ephesus. He knew there was no need to explain what sin was; they already knew. "You were dead in your sins, which you used to live in as you followed the desires of human nature," Paul wrote. He went on to explain how man is unable to change himself or make himself good enough to stand before a holy God. "All of us were guilty of sin, and none of us on our own could make ourselves holy enough for God. We were like dead men, caught in our own evils and waiting for the death sentence."

"But," Paul wrote in larger letters, "but then God, did something to save us from the penalty of our sins! Because of His great love for us, He acted in mercy and rescued us. Not only did He rescue us, but He allowed us to have new life in Christ! Remember it is only by God's grace that we have been saved through faith—and this faith is not even from ourselves; it also is the gift of God, in case anyone should boast!"

What is the difference between God's mercy and His grace? It has been said that mercy is not getting what we do deserve (punishment), while grace is getting that which we don't deserve (God's love).

Paul continued, reminding them of how they were once walking in the darkness of sin, but now walked by the light of God's will. "For we are God's workmanship, created in Jesus to do good works, which God has prepared in advance for us to do," he wrote.

Paul reminded them how they had been brought near to God only because of the blood of Christ. He reminded them of their hopelessness to help themselves. He reminded them of what God did for all mankind and what God offers to do in and through us.

"I pray for you that you might understand how wide and long and high and deep is the love of Christ," he wrote. "That you might know this love that goes beyond the greatest things you can imagine! To God, who is able to do more than anything we can ask or imagine, through His power which is at work in us—to God be the glory for ever and ever!"

Paul stood up to stretch as he lay his pen to the side of the parchment. He couldn't help but think of his own life and how he had been rescued from the darkness of sin. "Thanks be to God," he breathed with a sigh of relief.

CLIMBING ONWARD

Turn to Ephesians 2:4, 5. What does verse 4 tell us about God? According to verse 5, what did this cause Him to do for us?

Skill Time

Don't put your Bible aside! Turn to Ephesians 3:20-21. These verses are talking about God and His abilities. What is God able to do? He is able to do more than we can even think of or ask! Imagine that! Stop now and thank God for His character and what He has done for you.

Grow Up

TAKEN FROM EPHESIANS 4—5

Getting Ready

Ask God to examine your heart as you prepare to journey into His Word. Give Him permission to point out and help you change areas in your life where you need to grow.

The Journey

Has anyone ever said to you, "Why don't you just grow up!" How did you feel?

Paul had already explained the great spiritual blessings for those who know Jesus. He had reminded the believers in Ephesus of their sinful heritage, and all that God had done for them so they could come to know Him. Now he needed to remind them of one more thing.

"But to each one of us, God's grace has been given," Paul wrote. "We have been given gifts and abilities to use in building one another up, so we might all become more mature in Christ. We are not to be like babies, not knowing what we believe or why, but instead, we are to speak the truth in love and grow up in Christ."

Paul continued, explaining how believers are called "the body of

Christ" and how Christ is the head or leader. All believers come under Christ's leadership. Paul explained how a body is connected by ligaments and muscles that work together, so believers are to work together. As each believer does his or her part, the body grows and is built in love. The resulting unity acts as a thermometer of the body's maturity.

"Therefore," Paul challenged, "each one of you must put off falsehood of any kind and speak the truth to one another, for we are all members of one body. If you become angry at something or someone, do not let the sun go down on your anger. Instead, seek to make it right immediately. If you don't, a root of bitterness will spring up in your heart and it will give Satan a perfect foothold in your life," Paul warned.

A *foothold* is a place where one can stand and move around with confidence. Paul warns believers not to allow Satan to have a foothold in their life.

Paul's pen flowed across the parchment, leaving a trail of challenging words behind. "Do not let any unwholesome talk come out of your mouths," he wrote, "but only talk which is helpful for building up others. Let your words always be of benefit to those who hear them. Do not grieve the Holy Spirit by tuning Him out or by disobeying God, for you were sealed with the Holy Spirit until the day of redemption. Also, get rid of all bitterness, anger, fighting, back-talking, and other acts that are not honoring to God," Paul instructed.

"Instead, be imitators of God as dearly loved children. Live a life of love—Christ's kind of love, who loved us and gave Himself up for us. This kind of love is a love of actions. Don't be content to remain as a baby Christian; instead, grow and be made new in the attitude of your minds. Strive to become more like God in true righteousness and holiness."

Look up Ephesians 5:1, 2. What two commands sum up all that you just read? (Hint: there's one at the start of each verse.)

What best describes your goals in your spiritual walk? Are you remaining a baby or becoming an imitator of Christ? How do you know?

THIS MEANS WAR!

TAKEN FROM EPHESIANS 6

GETTING READY

Take a moment to look at the things around you. There's more to life than what you see—literally! Because we are human, we cannot see that which is spiritual with our eyes. Ask God to help you live in such a way that you never forget about the things you cannot see.

THE JOURNEY

If you were a soldier, would you have a hard time believing you were under attack if you couldn't see, feel, or hear the enemy?

"Finally, be strong in the Lord and in the power of His might!" Paul wrote as he closed his letter to the Ephesians. Being in prison, he had quietly observed all the pieces of armor Roman soldiers wore. Paul knew each piece had a special purpose so the soldier could stand against an attack from his enemy.

Before a Roman soldier put on his armor, he put a belt around his waist to hold his clothes together. This belt gave the soldier ability to move about freely and also became a place upon which he could hang his sword. Next came the breastplate, which protected the soldier's heart and vital organs from an attack. Sandals were important; they gave him the ability to go anywhere surefootedly. The shield a soldier carried was oblong and made of two pieces of wood glued together and covered with linen and leather. It was about two-and-a-half feet wide and four feet long! Because of the way the shield was made, fiery arrows would simply sink into the thick wood and be put out. The helmet the soldier wore was hot and uncomfortable and used only when facing danger. The only weapon a soldier carried for attacking was a sword—actually a short dagger. It was used in close-up battles.

Observing all this armor, Paul couldn't help but think of the protection God has given to each believer. "Put on the full armor of God so you can stand against Satan and his schemes," Paul wrote, comparing it to the soldier's armor. "Our struggle is not with an enemy we can see, but with an enemy we cannot see. It is not a war against flesh and blood, but against the powers and forces of Satan, the evil one who is at work in our world. Put on the armor of God so when you are attacked, you may be able to stand your ground."

Paul knew the believers must understand what God had equipped them with, so he compared spiritual armor to the Roman soldier's armor. He started with the belt, calling it "the belt of truth." Paul knew that as believers walked in truth and integrity, they would experience a great sense of freedom. They would experience God's power in their lives and would be able to use the sword (the Scriptures) kept at their side.

Next came the breastplate. Paul called this "the breastplate of righteousness." The person who stands in the righteousness of Christ and allows that to change his life, will be a person with a pure heart protected against evil.

The believer's feet should be protected with the Gospel—sure footing for all times.

Paul described the shield, calling it "the shield of faith." Only faith has the ability to protect a believer from the temptations (fiery arrows) and evil schemes of Satan's attacks.

Paul also compared salvation to pieces of armor, calling it "the helmet of salvation." Salvation provides a believer safety when facing death.

The sword is the Word of God—a deadly thing when used against Satan, and the only weapon that is able to put him in place.

"Put on the full armor of God," Paul told the believers, knowing that many would forget these things and attempt to stand in their own strength. "Pray on all occasions, and don't be afraid or ashamed to tell God about anything. Remember to pray for your Christian friends. Be on the alert and know the battle you are up against. Know and stand in the strength that God provides."

CLIMBING ONWARD

Turn to Ephesians 6:10, 11. What should you be strong in? How are you supposed to do that?

DANGER AHEAD

Satan is a defeated enemy, but only because of Christ's power. Don't try to fight the war in your own strength, for you will be defeated. Put on the armor God provides (know it, believe it, and act upon it), and you will be able to stand—and withstand—anything! God already has the victory.

GETTING YOUR BEARINGS:
THE BOOK OF PHILIPPIANS

Like Ephesians, the book of Philippians was also written by Paul while imprisoned in Rome. It was a letter written to believers in Philippi—a church that was started as a result of Paul's visiting there on his second missionary journey (Acts 16). As you may remember, while Paul was in jail at Philippi he sang hymns of praise to God and was miraculously delivered! The jailer saw all this, he and his household became believers in Christ. Lydia was a woman who sold purple fabric and after hearing the Gospel, she and her household believed as well! The church in Philippi was born.

This book was written ten years later. Upon hearing the news of Paul's imprisonment in Rome, the church of Philippi sent Epaphroditus (their pastor) to comfort Paul and to deliver a gift of money to make his stay in jail more comfortable. While visiting Paul, Epaphroditus became ill—almost to the point of death. When he became better he returned to Philippi, taking Paul's letter with him.

As you journey through Philippians, you will see that Paul's main reason for writing was to thank the Philippians for their concern. He also used this opportunity to write about a concern he had for them. It seems some in the church were thinking more highly of themselves than they ought. Others were doing right things for the wrong reasons, and wrong things with the right motives. It is some of these concerns and corrections that Paul includes in his letter to the believers in Phillipi.

LET ME PRAY FOR YOU

TAKEN FROM PHILIPPIANS 1

GETTING READY

Before you begin your journey today, ask the Lord to show you areas in your prayer life that need growth. Thank Him that He is a God who answers prayers.

THE JOURNEY

Are you ever at a loss for words and not sure what or how to pray when someone says, "Can you please pray for me?"

It was ten years since Paul had been in Philippi on his second missionary journey. Ten years, yet his love for them remained as if it were only yesterday. Epaphroditus had recently come with gifts from the Philippian believers and also reported on their well-being. Now, with pen in hand, Paul responded to their kindness and Epaphroditus's report.

"To all the believers in Philippi, God's grace and peace to you from our Lord Jesus Christ," Paul wrote as he began his letter. He introduced himself as a servant of Christ rather than his customary introduction as an apostle. The tone in his letter was one of love, and that seemed to flow from his heart, through his pen, and onto the parchment.

"Every time I think of you, I thank God. I have prayed many prayers for you and I always pray with great joy because of your part in receiving and sharing the Gospel. What's more, I have no doubt that God who began a good work in you will continue to work in your lives until the day of Christ.

"My thoughts toward you are full of love. Only the Lord Himself knows how deep my feelings are for you; for the love I have is a love which comes from God," Paul wrote as he sat back in his chair. He was so far away from them, yet he held them close to his heart!

"This is how I have been praying for you: I pray that your love may grow to overflowing so you may know more of God's love and show it to others. May you grow in knowledge and be able to understand God's ways better. In doing this, I pray you may be able to test everything that comes into your lives so you can choose what is best over that which is simply good. I also pray that you will be sincere and blameless; pure before God. As far as your fellow brothers and sisters in Christ, I pray that you will be able to get along with each other. May your lives be filled with the fruit of the Spirit, and may God be glorified because of the way you live for Him," Paul wrote, silently praying the words he wrote.

> **"The day of Christ"** is a phrase Paul often used to describe the time when Jesus will come back (as He promised) to take all the remaining believers with Him to heaven.

Paul had seen God do many miraculous things in and through his own life because of prayer. He knew by experience that many of the battles in the Christian's life are won while on the knees in prayer. Paul wanted the Philippian believers to know how he prayed for them. Perhaps they would take this example and pray for one another.

CLIMBING ONWARD

Turn to Philippians 1:6 and read it. Who is doing the work? You can stand confident because you do not stand alone. God began a good work in you and He will finish the job.

Skill Time

Make this a project of yours. For the next several days, secretly pray Paul's prayer for a member in your family. Sometimes God works in small, quiet ways, so don't expect to get out a ruler and measure progress. Remember, too, God is working in your life at the same time.

WHAT'S THE CATCH?

TAKEN FROM PHILIPPIANS 1—2

GETTING READY

As you begin today, stop and pray. Ask God to help you to change any wrong motives or attitudes you might have hiding in your heart.

THE JOURNEY

How do you respond when you know someone is doing something good, but they're doing it for the wrong reasons?

Paul wrote to thank the believers in Philippi and to remind them of his prayers for them. He continued writing, expressing his joy that Jesus was being preached among them—even though some were preaching Christ for the wrong reasons.

"I want you to know that because I am imprisoned in Rome, the Gospel has been spreading. I have not hesitated to tell everyone I come in contact with (soldiers included) about Jesus Christ. I've shared the Gospel with everyone, and now the whole palace guard and others believe. This is the reason God has allowed me to be here in prison. Many of you have been encouraged as you have heard what God is doing. I am thankful and do not mind living in this condition," Paul wrote.

Paul continued. "Some of you who were once timid about preaching the Gospel are now speaking out boldly. I praise God for this! You are speaking the Word of God more courageously and fearlessly than ever before. Others are preaching the Gospel out of envy, secretly hoping to stir up trouble and cause me greater difficulties."

Paul was talking about a few in the church who were envious of him. Paul was in trouble for preaching the Gospel, so, the more the Gospel spread, the more trouble Paul would be in they thought. Not caring for Paul, they preached the Gospel in order to stir up more trouble and add to Paul's suffering.

> To be self-centered is sin. An easy definition of sin is to look at the letter in the center of the word sin - I. Sin is simply when I get centered on myself.

The outward action of preaching the Gospel was a good thing, but it was being done for the wrong reasons. Instead of becoming bitter or demanding they stop, Paul was able to give thanks to God! "What does it matter if they try to cause me harm? The important thing is that Christ is being preached—and because of this I rejoice," he stated.

Concerned, Paul presented them with a challenge to become more like Christ by serving one another in love: "Don't just look out for your own interests, but look out for the interests of others. That is what Jesus did, and you should strive to be like Him in your attitudes. For even though Jesus is God, He humbled Himself and came to earth, taking the form of a human. When He did this, He set aside all His privileges and honor as God. He didn't demand His rights as God, but did what He did for us—even though it meant suffering, being mocked, misunderstood, and unappreciated. He did it anyway—and not for personal gain.

"Therefore, since Jesus (being God) could humble Himself to become a servant, how could we dare think we are above such things? No! We are not to be self-centered, doing things from wrong motives or for our own personal gain. Instead, let us have this same attitude of humility that was in Christ Jesus our Lord."

CLIMBING ONWARD

Check out Philippians 2:4, 5 in your own Bible. What does it say to do? This is a good practice that will keep your own motives pure—guaranteed!

DANGER AHEAD

Wrong motives are dangerous killers. They can easily ruin something that started out as good. They are silent and not easily detected. They are deadly. Don't allow them to be a part of your life.

I HAVE A DREAM . . .

TAKEN FROM PHILIPPIANS 3

GETTING READY

Stop and pray. Thank the Lord for His loving patience toward you. Ask Him to help you delight in Him more.

THE JOURNEY

Do you think it's bad to want to be cool or well-liked by others?

"Finally friends," Paul wrote with passion, "rejoice in the Lord! I don't mind repeating this, and will do it as often as necessary. Our confidence is not in what we are or what we can do, but our glory is in Christ Jesus and what He has done for us!" Paul was aware of Judaizers who felt their own self-importance and looked down on others. At this point, Paul compared himself to them as an example of not boasting.

"I put no confidence in my own achievements or standings, although I myself might be able to do so if I wanted," Paul admitted. "For, I am a pure-blooded Jew, circumcised on the eighth day—a day only *pure*-blooded baby Jews are circumcised. I can trace my family history back to Abraham, and I am from the tribe of Benjamin," Paul informed them. Anyone from the tribe of Benjamin was held in great honor and importance among the Jews, for Israel's first king came from this tribe.

Paul continued, carefully detailing his past and the things he used to glory in. "As for a Hebrew, I was born a Hebrew son of Hebrew parents. I was also a Pharisee, a member of the strictest group of Jews, strongly upholding the law of Moses. I was zealous for the old laws and gladly killed those who spoke against them or who followed Christ. In my own eyes, I was faultless about the keeping of Jewish religious laws," Paul stated. He paused, clearing his thoughts from his past.

"I want you to know, even though I have reason to think more highly of myself than the Judaizers, I count it all as trash when I compare it to the value of knowing Christ. Instead of making a place for myself in society, I am confident of the place Jesus has made for me in heaven. That is what really matters. Righteousness does not come from keeping the law or because of ones own importance, it comes through faith in Christ," Paul wrote.

In Greek races, runners did not compete in order to cross a finish line. Instead, they tried to be the first one to reach a wooden goal. Paul's goal was not wooden, it was Jesus, and his running was so he might come closer in order to know Him better.

He then continued, telling how he would rather know Christ than be known by others. "I don't look at myself as having already arrived, but one thing I do: I press on toward the goal for the greater prize of knowing Christ, for my real home is in heaven. I encourage you all the more to stand firm in the Lord, and do not put your mind on earthly things that really amount to nothing."

CLIMBING ONWARD

Find Philippians 3:7 and read it. What were Paul's reactions to the things that made him seem cool or more important than others? Now skip down to verse 11. What was Paul's prize?

THINKING on your FEET

In the race of life, what goal or prize are you competing for?

THINK ABOUT IT

TAKEN FROM PHILIPPIANS 4

GETTING READY

Before you finish your journey through Philippians, take a moment to think about the thoughts you've had so far today. Are your thoughts pleasing to God? Ask the Lord to help you in this area.

THE JOURNEY

Have you ever struggled with thoughts?— Thoughts you couldn't get out of your mind no matter how hard you tried?

Paul's letter was coming to a close. His final words to the Philippian believers were words of personal experience. They were words Paul tried, tested, and found to be true. They were words of comfort and help to those who read them.

"No matter what comes your way, rejoice in the Lord. Rejoice in the Lord always, for even though you may not know what is going on, the Lord is always near. When difficult times arise and you think everything is going against you, do not be anxious or fearful. Instead, trust God.

Pray and talk to God about everything. Petition Him by telling Him about your needs. Be thankful that you can come into His presence and that He is a God who cares. Don't be afraid to request specific things, for it is only when we come to God that He can truly help us. When you do these things, God's peace will comfort your hearts. It is a wonderful peace that words cannot describe!" Paul explained.

Paul thought about his own life. He had many opportunities to become worried, angry, and to have his feelings hurt. He had been lied about, made fun of, and tortured. It would be easy for him to think about these things and become bitter or to anxiously worry about how everything was going to work out. Paul chose not to be controlled by his thoughts and feelings, but rather to be in control of them.

Guard is a military term meaning to protect, to set a fortress around. Our *hearts* and our *minds* simply mean our "emotions" and our "thoughts."

"Whatever things are true (reliable); noble (worthy of respect); right (fitting to God's standards); pure (wholesome and not immoral); lovely (encouraging peace rather than conflict); admirable (building up rather than tearing down something or someone)—these are the type of thoughts you should have. These thoughts are the kind which are excellent and praiseworthy," Paul wrote.

Paul did not know how much longer he would be alive, and he desperately wanted the Philippian believers to understand the joy that is found in living for Christ. Even though there were times Paul was hungry or poor, there were also times he was fed and rich. He didn't let his circumstances control his amount of love for his Lord. "I have learned to be content in any and every circumstance," Paul wrote. He didn't let his circumstances control his thought life, either. Instead, Paul kept turning everything over to God. Paul explained, "I can do anything and everything through my God who gives me the strength!"

CLIMBING ONWARD

Read Philippians 4:6, 7. Notice the words "but in everything." What are you supposed to do with everything? If you do this, what does God's peace promise to do for you?

CROSS ROADS

Will you let your thoughts be filled with peace so they can guard your heart and mind in Christ Jesus, or will you let your thoughts turn your heart from Christ?

GETTING YOUR BEARINGS:
THE BOOK OF COLOSSIANS

The Book of Colossians is another one of Paul's letters written while he was a prisoner in Rome. Colossians is unique in that it was written to a group of believers in Colosse whom Paul had never even met! Where did these believers come from and how did they know Paul?

Apparently Paul had sent a man named Epaphras on his behalf to share the Gospel with those in Colosse. According to Paul, Epaphras was a dear fellow servant and a faithful minister of Christ. Epaphras shared the Gospel with the Colossians and started the church there. Then he came back to Paul and told of the Colossians' great love for the Lord.

Unfortunately, a false teaching had started in Colosse, which began affecting the believers. This false teaching talked about the need to follow Old Testament laws and ceremonies; it involved the worship of angels; it excluded many people; and worst of all, it denied that Jesus was God. This last teaching is what prompted Paul to write this letter which has some of the greatest verses about Christ's deity found anywhere in Scripture! Paul also wrote to challenge the believers to grow in their spiritual walk.

As you journey through Colossians, keep your eyes open to the practical things Paul told the believers that would cause them to grow in their walk with the Lord. Also notice how he took them back to their foundation and their roots.

Awesome!

TAKEN FROM COLOSSIANS 1—2

Getting Ready

As you begin your journey in Colossians, ask the Lord to open your heart to gain a better understanding of Jesus and your walk with Him.

THE Journey

If someone challenged you to name at least eighteen things that describe who Jesus is and what He does, could you? Try.

Paul's heart greatly rejoiced when Epaphras returned with news. The good news was that the believers in Colosse had a strong love for the Lord. The bad news was that a false teaching was spreading and Paul feared it would get into the church. This false teaching was of the worst kind—it actually denied the deity of Christ by saying Jesus was not really God! Such false teaching was known as heresy and the Colossian believers needed to be warned!

Paul quickly began his letter by telling how often he prayed for them since hearing of their love for the Lord. "Every time I pray, I do not forget to pray for you. I pray that God will fill you with the knowledge of His will through all spiritual wisdom and understanding. I pray that your life will be pleasing to Him in every way: that you may bear the fruit of the Holy Spirit, come to know God more, be strengthened with His power (so you won't give up in difficult times or seek revenge in times of anger), and be able to joyfully give thanks to God."

Not one to beat around the bush, Paul continued, reminding them of their roots and all Jesus is and had done. "Nothing compares with Christ and knowing Him! In Jesus, we have redemption and forgiveness for our sins. Jesus is the mirror–like image of God's qualities. He existed before creation. All things were created by Him in heaven and on earth. All things were created for His glory. Jesus is over all things, holds all things together, and is head of the church. He set the pattern for resurrection, and is to have first place in everything. In

Being rooted means to know your foundation, to dig in and stand on it, then to grow. Just as a plant without roots cannot grow, we cannot grow in our walk with God unless we're rooted in Jesus.

Jesus the fullness of God dwells. Through His blood we are made holy and able to have a relationship with God. Jesus gives us peace, presents us holy, and presents us without shame."

Paul knew that just knowing this was not enough. The believers in Colosse needed to stand on it to grow. "Just as you came to know Jesus, so live in His power. Be rooted and built up in Him as you were taught, and be strengthened in your faith. Keep your life overflowing with thankfulness for what Jesus has done for you. Don't let anyone trick you with empty religion or man's wisdom. Remember that when you were dead in your sins, God made you alive with Christ. Your sins have been forgiven because they were taken away and nailed to the cross. Only Jesus could do this for you, because in Him all God's deity dwells."

CLIMBING ONWARD

Turn to Colossians 2:6, 7. Verse 7 talks about being rooted, being built up, and growing in your faith. Verse 6 gives a beginning point. How and when does someone become rooted?

Skill Time

How and when were you rooted? Do you know a specific date when you asked Jesus to be your Lord and Savior? Since you gave your life to Jesus, are you being built up? How is your relationship with Jesus coming along? Take a few minutes to examine your heart. Then ask Jesus to help you in your walk with Him. There is so much He longs to do in and for you.

NEW AND IMPROVED

TAKEN FROM COLOSSIANS 3

GETTING READY

Pray, asking God to help you deal with some old thoughts and bad habits that keep dragging you down. Thank Him that He is able to give you the power and strength to change.

THE JOURNEY

Do you ever get distracted or taken in by what the world has to say or to offer?

Paul knew he could write more concerning who Jesus is and what He has done, but he didn't. Instead, he wrote about the next step.

"Since you have been raised with Christ, set your heart on Him, not on earthly things. For you have a new life in Christ. Consider yourself dead to your old nature and its sinful practices; your old nature is no longer your master. Things, such as anger (which is a smoldering hatred), sudden outbursts of rage, the desire to see others suffer, speaking evil of them, allowing filthy language to come from your lips, lying— these are all part of the old nature which should not control you."

Paul tapped his pen lightly on the parchment seeking the right words. "Just like taking off a dirty shirt, you have taken off your old self with its evil practices and put on the new self. This new self needs to be refreshed and renewed daily—and this only comes through getting to know Jesus better. The goal of the new self is to become more like Christ," Paul explained.

Paul knew the believers were tempted to behave just like those around them. Believers needed to know that such behavior was not fitting. Paul wrote, "Just as you are God's chosen people, separated for Him and dearly loved, you are to be different than the world and the world's standards. You are to clothe yourself with compassion (seeing the needs of others), and kindness (doing something about those needs). You should have humility and a gentle attitude toward others; be patient when angered and put up with others who don't show these qualities. Forgive the complaints you have against one another in the same manner that Christ has forgiven you. Allow God's peace to rule in your hearts and have an attitude of thankfulness. Let His Word dwell in you as you teach and encourage one another."

> In the Bible, behavior is often compared to wearing clothes! Behavior is what you choose to show yourself wearing. There are two standards for behavior: the world's and God's. Just as you sometimes judge others by their clothes, others judge you by your behavior.

Paul had written many specific things the Colossian believers should be doing. Since they had new life in Christ, they needed to live that new life in the here and now. They needed to grow. Only by making a decision to put off their old self and put on the new, could they have victory in their lives. This type of living would rise far above the world's standards.

"Whatever you do, whether actions or words, do it all in the name of the Lord Jesus," Paul summarized. He knew the greatest way to glorify God is through a changed life, and the greatest test of a believer's maturity is allowing himself to be changed.

CLIMBING ONWARD

Find Colossians 3:2. What does this verse challenge us to do?

CROSS ROADS

Are you living a new and improved life, or are you still living by the old self?

HEY, DIDN'T ANYONE NOTICE?

TAKEN FROM COLOSSIANS 3—4

GETTING READY

Spend a few minutes alone with God in prayer. Tell Him about your efforts of trying to live a life pleasing to Him. Ask Him to help you to continue to rely on His strength, and thank Him that He takes notice of you—even if no one else does.

THE JOURNEY

Does it frustrate you when others are recognized for some good things they did and you aren't? Why?

Paul continued writing as words flowed from his pen. He made a mental note of the territory he had already covered in his letter to the Colossian believers. Perhaps the greatest thing he did in the letter was to remind them of all that Jesus is and has done for them. Once they were reminded of that, Paul challenged them to continue to grow and live a life worthy of that calling. Now, it seemed, Paul was down to the last details; the important tidbits he didn't want them to forget.

"Make wise choices in the way you live. Be especially aware of your actions and the effect they might have on any non-believers. Live for

Jesus at every opportunity, even when it seems no one is paying much attention. You should live in such a way that you are always ready and able to talk about the Lord. Let your talk always be pleasing and your words pure and meaningful. If they are, they will be like salt and will cause others to thirst to know why you are different," Paul wrote.

Paul continued on, "Epaphras sends his greetings. He is always praying that you will stand firm in the will of God and that you will grow and mature."

The description of Epaphras's humble service was a description of how the growing believers were to act. Epaphras didn't pray for others because it brought him great recognition, appreciation, or praise! Until Paul mentioned it, no one had known what Epaphras was doing! Epaphras was an example of doing something out of love for God rather than for the praise of people. Paul used this as an example and a challenge. "Whatever you do, work at it with all your heart. Do it for the Lord rather than for people. It is the Lord Jesus whom you serve, and it is He who will reward you." Paul felt enough had been said. He added some final greetings, signed his name, and silently prayed that his words would find their mark.

Epaphras was a believer from Colossae who visited Paul while he was a prisoner in Rome. In Philemon 23, Paul called Epaphras his "fellow prisoner in Christ."

CLIMBING ONWARD

Turn to Colossians 3:23, 24. How are we to work? Read it again. God sees your deeds, and His rewards are great. Continue to do your work, even if it seems no one is noticing.

DANGER AHEAD

You will have many opportunities to secretly live your life for the praise and recognition of man. Don't. It only results in frustration, impure motives, and a temptation to give up. Don't let your heart fall into that trap! Instead, do your work for *God* and Him alone. Nothing ever escapes His notice—or His rewarding love.

GETTING YOUR BEARINGS:
THE BOOK OF I THESSALONIANS

If Paul's writings were put in the order they were written, Galatians would be first, followed by Thessalonians.

Paul wrote this letter to the church in Thessalonica, which started as a result of his second missionary journey. Acts chapter 17 provides an account. As you may remember, Paul had a vision of someone in the region of Macedonia calling out for help. Paul changed his travel plans and ventured into Macedonia, stopping at Philippi, the first major city in that region. Leaving Philippi, Paul followed the major Roman road, which led straight into the city of Thessalonica.

As was Paul's custom, he started preaching in the Jewish synagogues. His message was simple; proclaiming what the Old Testament taught about the Messiah who would suffer, die, and be resurrected. He went on to explain that Jesus fulfilled what the Old Testament said. Because of Paul's message, many Jews, Gentiles, and wealthy Thessalonian women became followers of Christ. This angered the non-believing Jews who started a riot against Paul. One thing led to another, and Paul was ordered to leave Thessalonica before he had a chance to finish his work.

Leaving Thessalonica, Paul traveled to Berea, bearing a great concern for the new believers he had left behind. Worried, Paul sent Timothy back to check on their well-being. Timothy rejoined Paul while he was in Corinth and gave his report. In response to this report, Paul sat down to write the letter we now know as I Thessalonians.

As you journey through I Thessalonians, see if you can discover what Paul encouraged the believers to do. Can you put your finger on any problems Paul might have been writing to correct?

It's Pleasing to Me

TAKEN FROM 1 THESSALONIANS 2

Getting Ready

As you begin your journey today, ask the Lord to speak to your heart. Ask Him to help you understand what He wants you to learn.

The Journey

What goes through your mind when you see flashy T.V. preachers?

Paul couldn't believe it! The non-believing Jews who had caused the riot forcing Paul to leave Thessalonica were now spreading misinformation and lies about him. They said Paul preached the Gospel only so he might live an easy life and fatten his wallet. They accused him of being a coward and a hypocrite since he had left in such a hurry! Paul felt sick at this report. That was the exact opposite of how he lived! Although these lies were personal attacks, Paul knew if they weren't corrected they would bring shame on the name of Christ. So, with pen in hand, he set out to write.

"You yourselves know our visit to you was not a failure. Even though we had been insulted in Philippi and suffered, we still dared to tell you the Gospel in Thessalonica. We did not preach from impure motives or use flattery to cover up greed. For we were not trying to please men, but God! As apostles of Christ, we could have lived off your hard-earned money, but we did not. Instead, we lived in a gentle way among you, looking out for your needs. We not only preached the Gospel among you, but we also worked day and night, earning our own living so we would not burden anyone," Paul reminded them. He knew he had gone above and beyond what was necessary—even denying himself privileges and rights he had as a missionary—in order to live as an example among them. Even then there were false preachers who went around living off whomever they could. Paul had determined to live in such a way that he could never be confused with one of them. Paul's life was not one of taking, but of giving. He was not flashy, coming with false motives, but rather his motives were pure. He did not gain, but actually suffered for the sake of spreading the Gospel.

A correct definition of ministry is "doing God's work, God's way." Paul's life was an example. It has also been said that ministry is being God's person at God's time in the life of another person.

Paul continued on, challenging the believers to remember the example of how he lived his life among them. He not only lived it, but he also urged them to live in a manner worthy of God. He reminded them of how they accepted the Gospel not merely as man's words, but as God's message. The Thessalonians knew Paul's sudden leaving was not out of choice, but out of persecution and an order to leave. Paul brought them back to that fact and encouraged them to live blamelessly for Christ just as he had striven to do while he was with them.

CLIMBING ONWARD

Turn to I Thessalonians 2:4. How are you able to live a blameless life? Who should you strive to please? Why?

DANGER AHEAD

There are some who preach God and go into ministry for impure motives or personal gain. They set bad examples and often hurt the cause of Christ. Carefully examine their lives; don't be fooled—their ministry may not be of God.

Now That's Really Livin'

TAKEN FROM I THESSALONIANS 3

Getting Ready

Stop and pray. Preparing your heart is not just a to- do thing like tying your shoes. It is your time to talk to God and His time to get your attention so He can talk to you.

THE JOURNEY

What brings you the greatest joy and satisfaction in your life? What makes you feel like you're really living?

Paul looked at the parchment spread in front of him. Having dealt with the false things, now it was time to deal with the truth! Since being forced to leave Thessalonica in a hurry, Paul was only able to give the new Thessalonian believers a small amount of teaching. His concerns grew for them, he knew they would no doubt face the same persecution he had faced. Would they be able to stand? Did they have enough teaching so they could at least begin to grow? What would happen to the new church?

These were concerns Paul had, and they all seemed to vanish upon Timothy's arrival and report. It was with great joy that Paul wrote the next section of his letter, admitting the worry and concern he had for them.

"I had wanted to come to you again and again, but was prevented from doing so! When I could stand it no longer, I sent Timothy to strengthen and encourage you in your faith, for we did not want you to be unsettled by trials. Even when we were with you, we kept saying that persecution would come, and so it did, as you well know. Out of concern for your well-being, I sent Timothy to find out about your faith. There was a fear in my heart that perhaps the tempter might have tempted you in some way and that our work among you might have been destroyed. But, that is not the case!" Paul wrote. The gleam in his eyes reflected his thankfulness to God.

"Unsettled by trials"— the word *unsettled* is the same word used to describe a dog's tail wagging back and forth. Paul feared the new believers would go back and forth in their faith because of the trials they were facing.

"Even though we were followed by troublemakers and had angry crowds stirred up against us, we have great encouragement because we hear about your faith. Word has gone out about how you not only turned from idols to serve a living and true God, but also continued on, even in the face of persecution, to stand firm in your faith. This is great encouragement to us! We can think of no greater blessing or joy! For now we really live, since you are standing firm in the Lord! How can we thank God enough for the great joy we have in Him because of you?" Paul wrote, expressing the feelings in his heart.

Paul continued, telling how the Thessalonian believers were in his prayers both day and night. "May the Lord make your love overflow for one another, just as our love overflows for you." He prayed for their hearts to be strengthened and made blameless—so they would deal with their sin as God requires and no one could charge them of any wrong doing. He prayed that they would be holy; separated for God's use. Paul's joy was not in what he had done among them. His joy was in the fact that he could see God working in their lives.

246

CLIMBING ONWARD

Find I Thessalonians 3:8, 9 in your Bible. What brought Paul satisfaction?

Skill Time

Think of the people in your life who have made an impact on you spiritually (parents, teachers, youth group leaders, friends, etc.). Does your life cause them joy? Select one person and write them an encouragement note telling them how they have touched your life, and thank them for it. Mail it today.

100% PURE — GUARANTEED

TAKEN FROM I THESSALONIANS 4

GETTING READY

As you begin your journey in God's Word today, ask Him to speak to you. Give Him permission to point out areas in your life that are not honoring to Him. Ask Him to help you live by His rules.

THE JOURNEY

Do you ever feel God's rules and guidelines are only meant to destroy your fun?

Paul knew of the many ungodly influences in the city of Thessalonica. Although there was a strong Jewish synagogue, the main group of people in Thessalonica were Greek. The Greeks were very open and loose in their living. Part of their religion actually included acts of immorality! It was considered nothing to be sexually intimate with anyone and everyone, and some were using their bodies in ways God never intended.

Paul was aware of this destructive influence and wanted to encourage the new believers in Thessalonica to be on their guard. They needed to love God with a whole heart and strive to live in ways pleasing to Him. "We instructed you how to live a God-honoring life, just as you are now doing, and need to do all the more. For our instructions come not from ourselves, but from the authority of the Lord," Paul wrote. He knew God's rules were to protect them so they could experience life in the most meaningful way, rather than accepting the world's cheap substitute.

"Each of you should learn self-control and how to control your own body in a way that is holy and honorable. Those who do not know God allow their lives to be ruled by sexual desires. They do immoral acts because they want something their way instead of God's. They think they are gaining everything, when really they are missing out. They dishonor not only themselves, but the others they involve in their sin. They hurt themselves, wrong the other person, and sin against God. God will punish them for such sins. You, however, are to live a life of purity. God called you to live a holy, purposeful, and satisfied life. God's rules are for your benefit and personal growth," Paul instructed.

> Sexual impurity (or immorality) is doing sexual things now, that God says should be saved for marriage. It is also doing such things with others instead of your marriage partner.

Paul tapped his pen on the parchment and thought for a moment. The pen was soon in motion again, as Paul challenged them to lead a peaceful life, not one ruled by desires, passions, or circumstances. The believers needed to examine their own lives, making sure they were following the will of God, rather than comparing or examining others' lives. They were to set a good example of working, rather than depending on others to provide for them. This type of living would show the purity in their hearts. This type of living would show their love and commitment to following God's rules. God's rules and guidelines weren't to destroy fun, they were meant to protect people from destroying themselves.

Look up I Thessalonians 4:7, 8. What is the purpose of God's loving guidelines? What happens if we reject them?

Skill Time

What will you do when temptation for impurity comes knocking at your door? Pull out the card of I Corinthians 10:13 that you made while journeying through Corinthians. If you lost it, make another one. Review the verse and commit it to memory now, if you didn't earlier. Notice the words "God is faithful and provides a way of escape."

Next time you are in a tempting situation, look for God's exit (He always provides one) and leave!

WHO? WHAT? WHEN?

TAKEN FROM I THESSALONIANS 4—5

GETTING READY

Things in life don't always happen when we want or expect. Spend a few minutes thinking about God's timing. Thank the Lord that He is in control and His timing is perfect.

THE JOURNEY

Have you ever wondered how and when Jesus will come back?

In Paul's day, people believed that the evil spirits lived in the air between heaven and earth. The air was Satan's territory—his turf. Because of this, Satan has been called "the Prince of the power of the air." When Jesus comes back again, believers will rise to meet the Lord in the air—Satan's turf! This great reunion with Jesus will take place in Satan's territory, marking a sting of defeat for Satan while proclaiming Jesus' triumphant victory. When will all this happen?

"Be ready!" Paul warned, "For the Lord Himself will come from heaven with a shout; with the voice of the archangel and with the trumpet call of God. The believers who are dead in Christ will rise first. Then, we who are still alive will be caught up together with them to meet the Lord in the air. We will then be with the Lord forever!"

Paul knew the Thessalonians had questions concerning this. They had been taught that Jesus promised to return and they desired to know when this would take place. Paul knew there was danger in knowing. People who think they have all the time in the world become caught up in pleasing themselves and do not care about the future. They become foolish. Those who don't know the time of the Lord's return are more watchful, living to make their days count, not knowing if today will be their last. That is how believers are to live—daily looking forward to the Lord's return. The day of the Lord is something no person has the privilege of knowing. God, who knows man's character and weaknesses, planned it that way—no one could possibly calculate days or claim to be wise enough to figure it out.

Today people use clever charts based on historical events and fulfilled prophecies, hoping to predict the day of Jesus' return.

Paul continued to write, "The time and date this happens we cannot tell you, for Jesus Himself said no one would know. Rather, the day of the Lord will be like a thief in the night. It will come when people least expect it, suddenly, unplanned for, and by surprise. Therefore, be alert and self-controlled. Encourage others to do the same and build each other up," Paul instructed.

The time when Jesus returns is a time which is at God's pleasure. God planned it that way—to protect us against ourselves! Jesus (who) will return (what), at a time only God knows (when).

CLIMBING ONWARD

Find I Thessalonians 5:2 in your Bible and read it. What does it say? Now, turn back to Mark 13:32, 33 and read Jesus' own words concerning this.

DANGER AHEAD

Although It Is clear to see that the time of Jesus' coming is drawing ever near, this is all that is clear. No one could (or should) be so bold as to say they have God's timetable figured out. To do so would be to call God a liar, for He specifically says no man shall ever know. (Reread Jesus' words in Mark 13:32, 33.)

You will undoubtedly hear people make predictions on when Jesus will come back. They might even use charts and a handful of Bible verses or fulfilled prophecies to support their views. Don't get caught up in their foolish predictions. It will only lead to disappointment and distract you from living for Him each day that He gives you here on earth.

YOU LOOK A LITTLE GREEN

TAKEN FROM I THESSALONIANS 5

GETTING READY

As you finish your journey through I Thessa-loni-ans, take a few minutes to think about the new Thessalonian believers and their need for growth. Thank the Lord for growth in your life and ask Him to help you to live according to His will.

THE JOURNEY

If someone asked you for advice on how to grow spiritually and live according to God's will, what would you say?

Paul knew his last words would be important—last words are usually remembered the most. Paul paused a moment, as if to sum up every-thing.

"Respect the spiritual leaders who are over you. They work hard in your behalf and should be loved and held in highest regard. Listen to what they say, for they are responsible to God for your care," Paul instructed.

"Continue to live at peace with one another, not stirring up fights or problems. I urge you to warn those who neglect their daily duties, encourage those who are easily discouraged, strengthen those who haven't yet learned to lean on the Lord as they should, and be patient with everyone. Don't pay back wrong with wrong, but purpose in your heart to be kind to everyone. This can be done only through God's love working in and through you," Paul wrote. He then became more specific about God's will for them.

The Thessalonians were new believers. They were on the right track and doing a good job, but needed to push onward and grow in their walk with the Lord. Paul's words challenged their attitudes and personal lives before God.

"Be joyful always," Paul wrote. "Rejoice in the blessings of Jesus, rather than depending on circumstances.

"Pray continually," Paul challenged, reminding the believers to talk with God throughout the day. This meant that they should include God in everything and talk with Him like a good friend.

"Give thanks in every circumstance," Paul instructed. "Giving of thanks shows trust in God. It accepts both the good and the bad, trusting that Jesus knows what He is doing."

Paul then gave a warning: "Do not ignore the Holy Spirit's teaching in your life. When He puts it in your heart to do something, do it. Test everything that comes your way to make sure it is in line with what the Scriptures say. Hold onto that which is good and avoid every kind of evil."

Having said all that, Paul finished his letter with a prayer. "May God continue to change you into what He wants you to be. May you continue to grow in your walk with Him, so your life is blameless and full of honor until the coming of our Lord Jesus Christ. God who calls you is faithful, and He will do it."

CLIMBING ONWARD

Turn to I Thessalonians 5:23, 24. As you do your part, God works in your life and He causes the growth. When is the work completed?

CROSS ROADS

If you could compare life to living in a vegetable garden, you would be aware of a simple law of nature: "If you think you're green, you'll grow; if you think you're ripe, you'll rot!" In your walk with the Lord, do you think you're ripe or do you still consider yourself green? Why?

GETTING YOUR BEARINGS:
THE BOOK OF II THESSALONIANS

Second Thessalonians was written within a year after Paul wrote I Thessalonians. The reason for his second letter to the believers was to praise them for their continued spiritual growth and to correct a false teaching concerning the the day of the Lord. Paul not only corrected this bad teaching, but he also warns the believers of the consequences of it.

YOU MEAN, WORK?

TAKEN FROM II THESSALONIANS 3

GETTING READY

Before you journey, think about your attitude toward chores, jobs, or just plain work. Ask God to help you have a better attitude in this area.

THE JOURNEY

Do you know where the phrase, "If you don't work; you don't eat!" came from?

Why should I bother doing that?! If Jesus is coming back at any time then it really doesn't make much difference if I do this or not! thought some of the believers. Due to some incorrect teaching they began thinking the wrong way. "Quit your jobs! The Lord is returning tomorrow!" was the false message. Many didn't think their work made much difference if the end of the world was coming. So instead of working, they simply gave up and stopped working. "We'll just wait for Christ's return," they lazily told themselves. Others believed Jesus had already returned and were confused. In the midst of all this, there were some lazy believers who merely watched others work, then came around asking for favors and food. In his first letter, Paul challenged them to work, but apparently the idle people had not obeyed. With this false teaching, conditions were even worse! All this created great difficulties and became an issue Paul needed to address.

"You remember how we lived among you when we were there. We did not eat anyone's food without paying for it, nor did we just take from others. Instead, we worked hard and earned our keep. Even though we had the privilege as missionaries to be supported by you, we did not become a burden. Instead, we lived as an example for you to follow," Paul began. His words turned more serious as he thought of those who were living off the hard work of others.

Idle means unmoving, lazy, not going anywhere or doing anything. Sometimes this word is used to describe a car whose engine is running, but the car is out of gear and not going anywhere.

"We have heard there are some who are idle. Instead of being busy with their own responsibilities, they are busybodies, interfering in the business of others. I instruct you, keep away from them. They must learn to earn the bread they eat; they must learn to work. Do not associate with them in order that they may feel ashamed and turn from their ways. Don't regard them as an enemy, but do this to warn them as a brother," Paul instructed.

"As for you, follow the example we set. Never tire of doing what is right," Paul encouraged. He knew it was difficult to keep working hard when others who are lazy seem to do as well, if not better! "Keep working hard, remember our example to you, and live by the standard that God has set for us: "If a man will not work, he shall not eat.""

Look up II Thessalonians 3:11. What does it say? Who does it describe?

Describe yourself. Are you a busybody or are you busy? In what ways?

GETTING YOUR BEARINGS:
THE BOOK OF I TIMOTHY

First Timothy is one of Paul's letters known as a pastoral letter or epistle. It is counsel, advice, and encouragement given to Paul's coworkers who were serving as leaders (pastors) in the regions of Crete and Ephesus. Timothy was one of those coworkers and became Paul's closest friend to the very end.

When Paul was on his first missionary journey, he went to Derbe where young Timothy lived. Timothy was around eighteen or nineteen when he heard Paul's message and became a believer. When Paul revisited Derbe on his second missionary journey, he saw great promise in Timothy and took him on as an assistant. Timothy traveled with Paul and did small tasks. Before long, Timothy became a coworker in sharing the Gospel message. Timothy stayed behind to work with new believers in one area while Paul traveled on to other areas. Timothy was a loyal, trusted friend who even became Paul's companion in prison.

As you may remember from the close of Acts, Paul was left imprisoned in Rome. He had spent many years traveling on his missionary journeys only to return to Jerusalem and be thrown in prison for preaching the Gospel message. It took him five years to work his way through the Roman court system, which eventually brought him to Rome (where Acts leaves off).

By piecing together information from Paul's other letters, we discover that Paul was released after two years of imprisonment in Rome. Paul took Timothy and went on a journey to revisit the churches he had started on his earlier missionary journeys. After visiting Ephesus, Timothy is left behind to provide much-needed leadership while Paul traveled on to visit other churches. In I Timothy Paul wrote to Timothy, checking how things were going. It is a personal letter full of love, instruction, and encouragement.

As you journey through I Timothy, see if you can find what Paul had to say to Timothy about: sound teaching, prayer, leadership, personal godliness, and contentment.

IN MY OPINION

TAKEN FROM I TIMOTHY 1

GETTING READY

Pray, thanking God that His Word is truth and His ways are right. Thank Him that He has called you into His kingdom.

THE JOURNEY

Do you think everyone who talks about religion has a serious interest in God?

"Is not!"
"Is too!"
"Is not!"
"Is too!"
"Well, in my opinion . . ."

Some in Ephesus were getting involved in discussions and arguments that led nowhere. They delighted in debating over fables, family histories, and even religious teachings different from those that Paul taught. Everyone had an opinion, and each thought her own opinion was right. Believers were arguing only to prove who was right and who was wrong, and their discussions were over things that didn't even matter!

Instead of being built up, people were becoming confused. The arguing was pointless and unproductive. It had nothing to do with sound doctrine (God's truth).

"Timothy," Paul wrote, "continue to stay in Ephesus and command those who are teaching different doctrines to stop. They are causing arguments and confusion. They do not promote God's work, which is by faith."

Paul continued writing, "I am aware that some have wandered away from a pure heart, a good conscience, and a sincere faith. Leaving God's truth behind, they turn instead to meaningless talk. Wanting to be teachers of the law, they do not know what they are talking about or what they pretend to agree with. They only teach and argue so they might believe themselves to be important and more knowledgeable than others."

Sound doctrine is not a term used to describe noise. *Sound* means "that which is right." It is solid, firm, sure, true, trustworthy. The word *doctrine* simply refers to the foundation and building blocks of what we believe. It is the facts our faith is built upon.

"Timothy," Paul encouraged, "fight the good fight. Hold on to the solid teaching of God's truth, for this is what real faith is built upon. As you anchor yourself on God's sound doctrine, you will be able to maintain a clear mind."

Paul paused a moment before penning words of warning. "As you know, some have rejected God's truth and as a result, they have suffered shipwreck in their faith," he wrote. "Therefore, Timothy, stand firm and do not allow empty arguments and foolish teachings to be found among the believers."

Turn to I Timothy 1:5. What three things are important to faith? Skip down and read verse 17. Who receives the honor for this faith?

Skill Time

Many talk of God when they really know little about Him. Some talk about God as if He were a hobby. They are looking for someone they can confuse, disturb, or tear down with questions that seem unanswerable. Don't get trapped in their foolish arguments, but stand firm on God's truth. If you have opportunity to talk with someone like this, present the Gospel and leave it there. Don't try to win the person over by arguing or debating. Our strength is not in our own clever arguments, but in the Lord and the power of His Word! As God brings this person to mind, faithfully pray for him or her and then leave the rest in God' hands.

GOD BLESS

TAKEN FROM I TIMOTHY 2

GETTING READY

Before journeying into God's Word today, think about prayer for a moment. Ask God to show you His plan in praying for others and the benefits to those who take time to do so.

THE JOURNEY

Have you ever stopped to pray for our president and the leaders of our nation—even if you may not care for them?

Nero, the emperor of Rome, turned cruel toward the end of his reign. He did many bad things and blamed them on Christians. He tortured people—Christians being his favorite victims. Many people said he was a madman, but Paul said he was worthy of prayer. He was not worthy because of who he was or what he accomplished. Nero was worthy because God placed him in leadership over the people as a ruler.

"Timothy," Paul continued in his letter of encouragement and instruction, "I urge that prayers be made for everyone. This includes kings and all those in authority." Paul knew this would be difficult for many believers to do, so he went on to explain.

"God placed men in authority over us and He is in control. Just like all men, these leaders need God, and we must see their need for Him and pray in their behalf. We are to pray for them and thank God for them," Paul wrote.

"When we pray, for our leaders, we benefit. As God answers our prayers for them, we will be able to continue to live peaceful and quiet lives in all godliness and holiness," Paul instructed. "I want people everywhere to lift up holy hands in prayer without anger or arguing."

Check out I Timothy 2:1-4. What does it say about prayer? What does it say about God?

Skill Time

Praying for our nation's leaders is important. You may never know how your prayers are answered, but rest assured, God answers prayer! God desires for all men to be saved and come to the knowledge of truth. When you pray for national and local government leaders, you are praying something you know is in line with God's desires. Spend the next few minutes specifically praying for our president. Pray also for the governor of your state.

TO BE OR NOT TO BE

TAKEN FROM I TIMOTHY 3

GETTING READY

Stop and pray. Ask God to help you understand His point of view on leadership. Thank Him for His standards.

THE JOURNEY

In your opinion, what type of person makes a good leader?

Paul knew Timothy was facing many things in the large church at Ephesus. Questions concerning the choosing of leaders would soon surface. How would leaders in the church be picked? Who would make a good leader? Says who?

"I am writing you these things," Paul explained in his letter, "so you will know how people ought to behave in God's household." Paul used the word, household, to describe the church, for all believers are part of God's family. The church is made up of those who believe in Jesus; it is not the building in which believers worship. For now, however, Paul was going to liken the church to a building.

"The church of the living God is the pillar and foundation of the truth," Paul wrote, knowing that the Ephesians had a great understanding of pillars. It was in their city that one of the seven wonders of the world, the Temple of Artemis, was located. This temple was built to honor the false god Artemis and was known for its many pillars. One hundred and twenty-seven pillars—made of marble, studded with jewels, and overlaid with gold—caught the attention of everyone for miles around! Paul said the church is the pillar and supporter of the truth. Just like the pillars of the Temple of Artemis could be clearly seen, the church is to present the truth in all its glory to be clearly seen by others. Paul knew this could only be accomplished as godly leaders in the church influenced and encouraged other believers. For this reason, Paul included the topic of leadership in his letter to Timothy.

The Greeks believed Artemis was the god of hunting, nature, and the moon.

"The choosing of leaders in the church should not be based on popularity or talent," Paul instructed. "Instead, it should be by God's standards. According to God, leaders are to be self-controlled and not quarrelsome. They are to be respected and sincere in their words and actions. They must be able to get along with their family, otherwise, how could they get along with others in the family of God? A leader must be able to teach others and also be willing to learn. He should not be a lover of money, but rather be able to use what he has to serve others. These are the qualifications of a good leader," Paul wrote.

Paul's words of instruction clearly showed that leaders were not to be picked because of their abilities. They were to be picked because of their character. They were not to be picked by man's measure; they were to be picked by God's standards. Such leaders would help and encourage believers to be the pillar and supporter of the truth throughout the world.

CLIMBING ONWARD

Turn to I Timothy 3:5 and read it. What does it say? Why do you think this is so important? Managing one's own family describes the ability to get along with the family. It involves giving respect and being respected. There is a saying which states: The rules you live by privately (in your home) will determine how you will live publicly (in front of others). Or, put more simply, what you are like at home is what you are really like. Leaders need to be of proven character.

THINKING on your FEET

If you were standing in line to be measured up by God's standards of leadership, why would you be picked to be a leader?

And Now for Exhibit A

TAKEN FROM I TIMOTHY 4

Getting Ready

Take a moment to think about your life and the example you set. Is it a good example or one that needs a little work? Tell God your answer to this question. Ask Him to help you in the areas you are weak.

The Journey

Have others mocked you or made fun of you because you try to live a life that is honoring to God?

Paul knew he had given Timothy a big job. Being the leader of the church in Ephesus was no small task! Also, Timothy was considered young for his responsibilities and prone to being timid and fearful. Paul's next words were written to be of special encouragement to Timothy.

"Timothy," Paul wrote, "stand strong in the teachings and truth of the faith in which you were trained. Continue to teach these truths as you have been doing, and have nothing to do with the godless myths and old wives' tales that some are teaching. Instead, train yourself to be godly, and continue to live a life that is honoring to Him."

Paul specifically used the word *train* so Timothy would be reminded of the many athletes who spent time disciplining their bodies for a specific goal. Timothy's goal was that of godliness. Paul knew physical training was good, but it was also limited. Physical training could develop only part of the man, and its effects lasted for just a short while. Training in godliness, however, develops the whole person—body, soul, and mind. It is good not only for this life, but also for the life to come. Paul made careful note of that to Timothy.

Paul continued, "You have put your hope in the living God who is the Savior of all men. Continue to spread this message, and don't let anyone look down on you because you are young," Paul wrote. "Instead, be an example for the believers in your words, in your actions, in love, in faith, and in purity."

In Paul's day, the word *youth* was used to describe anyone of military age—age 40 or under.

Paul knew the church sought to have leaders who were over fifty. It was believed that until a person reached this age, they weren't mature enough to lead and set an example for others to follow. Paul told Timothy not to feel timid because he was only a youth. Instead, he was to show his maturity by living a godly life as an example to others. No matter what others said or thought, Timothy was to stand firm and to live for His Lord.

ook up I Timothy 4:12. According to this verse, how should you handle those who look down on you? In what five areas can you be an example?

Skill Time

On an index card or piece of paper, list the five areas you read about in verse 12. Think of a practical way you can be an example in each of these areas, and write it down next to the word. (Example: Speech—I will not talk back to my parents when I disagree with them.) For one week, practice the things you listed, keeping your list handy as a reminder.

I'M CONTENT

TAKEN FROM I TIMOTHY 6

GETTING READY

Ask God to speak to your heart and help you become more godly in your hopes and desires.

THE JOURNEY

How do you feel when you notice kids making fun of others because their clothes aren't the right brand or their house isn't big or cool? Has this ever happened to you?

This was the close of Paul's letter to Timothy, and he was ending it with the same concerns as when he began! "If people teach anything that is not of our Lord Jesus Christ, they are teaching false doctrine. Not only that," Paul stated, "they are conceited and only love arguing spiritual matters so they can pretend to know about God. Their real love is the love of controversies and quarrels. They stir up arguments and doubts that cause friction. These false teachers are filled with pride and are completely empty of God's truth. They think they can gain something or become rich by acting godly! How little they know!"

Paul knew that those who are truly godly don't demand riches for themselves. They don't look for what they can gain, but rather what they can give. They understand that their possessions are not their life. They are completely satisfied and content with God alone, even if it means not having anything else! Godliness doesn't lead to great gain, godliness itself is gain.

Paul continued, warning about the dangers of loving money. "The love of money is the starting point of all kinds of evil," he stated. "Some, who were eager for money or the promise of having the best of everything, have wandered from the faith. Their lives have been torn apart by the very things they sought."

> "Godliness" means acting the way Jesus would act and doing the things He would do. It is the act of becoming more like Him.

"Timothy," Paul wrote, "as a man of God, you must flee all this and strive after righteousness, godliness, faith, love, endurance, and gentleness. Command those who do have riches and nice possessions not to be proud or arrogant. They are not to put their hope in what they own, for it is uncertain and won't last. Instead, they are to put their hope in God who provided those things for them. They are to use their possessions as God-given things to enjoy and use to benefit and build up others. They are to be rich—not with things they have or own—but in good deeds. They are to be content, generous, and willing to share, knowing that God is the One who meets their needs."

CLIMBING ONWARD

Turn to I Timothy 6:17. What are two dangers for people who are rich? What should they fix their hope on? Why? Is your hope on things you hope to get, or is your hope in God?

Skill Time

Take the contentment challenge, and check your level of godliness! First, grab a piece of paper and pen, and write down three things that describe who you are and what you like. Then, walk into your bedroom, look around, and add at least four other things to your list that might distinguish you from others. Now, examine your list. Does it revolve around your character or around your possessions?

GETTING YOUR BEARINGS:
THE BOOK OF II TIMOTHY

Second Timothy was written under different circumstances than Paul's first letter to Timothy. In II Timothy Paul was back in Rome as a prisoner for preaching the Gospel, only this imprisonment wasn't like the first one. During Paul's first imprisonment, he was in a rented house under the guard of soldiers (sort of like being grounded by your parents!). This was called "house arrest."

Now, however, Paul was in a dark and damp dungeon. He had appeared before the wicked emperor, Nero, and the outlook was not good. Knowing death was a certain thing, Paul wrote what would be his last epistle (letter), and addressed it to Timothy. This letter contains Paul's last words of instruction, warning, and encouragement to Timothy.

As you journey through this book, notice Paul's love and concern for others despite his own circumstances. See how he encouraged Timothy and the believers to remain faithful to God even in the face of hardship.

HERE I STAND

TAKEN FROM II TIMOTHY 1

GETTING READY

As you begin to journey through II Timothy, think about your walk with God. Are you experiencing His joy and peace? If not, ask God to show you why, and give Him permission to change and rearrange things in your life.

THE JOURNEY

Is it easier to run from tough times or to stand and face difficulties?

The dark and dampness seemed to surround Paul like a death grip, threatening to choke out any remaining hope. Paul was in a Roman dungeon, awaiting execution. Despite his circumstances, Paul's thoughts were on things greater than his own difficulties. With a pen in hand he set out to write his final words to Timothy.

"Paul, an apostle of Jesus Christ by the will of God," he boldly wrote, never regretting or wishing it were otherwise. "May God's grace, mercy, and peace be with you. I thank God as I constantly remember you in my prayers. How I long to see you!" Paul's heart was anxious to see Timothy before winter. It seemed almost everyone had abandoned him and he was very lonely. Only Luke and Onesiphorus were not ashamed of Paul's chains. They had searched for Paul in Rome at their own risk—it was dangerous to be associated with a criminal.

Paul continued his letter, encouraging Timothy to remember his training in godliness and to depend upon the gifts and abilities God had given him to accomplish His work. "For God does not want us to be cowards, but to be confident and resting in the power, love, and self-discipline He gives us."

Paul knew Timothy might feel ashamed at having to defend a prisoner. He might also become fearful of proclaiming the message of the Gospel. Paul did not want this to happen. "Don't be ashamed of the message about our Lord, or of me a prisoner for His sake. Rather, join me in suffering for His cause. In times like these we can know and experience the power of God. God called us to be holy (not by our own works and efforts), but according to His will and grace. This was God's plan from the beginning of eternity and has been made known to us through Jesus who destroyed death and gave us the ability to live forever with God."

Why was Paul in jail again? On July 19, 64 A.D. Rome went up in flames. Many suspected Nero (who had become a madman) to have done it. Nero simply blamed the Christians. As a result, anyone who was a believer and proclaimed Christ was viewed and tried as a criminal in Rome.

Paul continued, "It is for this reason I suffer, but I am not ashamed. I know whom I have believed and I know for certain that He is able to take care of all that concerns my life." Paul knew no matter what happened, he could stand on the fact of the Gospel and God's character. Paul trusted God even in spite of hardship and difficult times. Paul's concern was that Timothy would stand firm too, having his courage rooted in God—that he would follow Paul's example, hold fast, and remain unashamed to testify about the Lord.

CLIMBING ONWARD

Look up II Timothy 1:12. What does Paul know? What does he say he is convinced of? This is something Paul personally experienced in his life and found to be true. Notice how he says I know *whom* I have believed not *what*. Paul could stand firm because of his personal relationship with God.

DANGER AHEAD

Tough times will come. At some point in your life, it may become life—threatening to be known as a Christian! The only way through difficult times is relying on your personal relationship with God. Know Him and experience His faithfulness now so that you will be able to stand confident in times of trouble.

I Can Handle It

TAKEN FROM II TIMOTHY 2

Getting Ready

Take a few moments to really talk with God. Share with Him what is on your heart and mind at this moment. Ask Him to take away your concerns or any bad attitudes so you can have a clear mind and pure heart that He can teach.

THE Journey

If you were to describe someone who is a good example of a believer in Christ, what would you describe?

Be strong. . . . be strong. . . . be strong! These were words that kept flooding Paul's mind and words that found their way onto the parchment. "Be strong in the grace that is in Christ Jesus," Paul stated. "Not only be strong in His grace, but teach faithful men about Him so they can teach others. Don't be afraid to suffer difficult times with me as a good soldier of the Lord."

Paul knew about soldiers, since he had spent much time in their company! He used this knowledge to help him describe what a believer in Christ should be like. "No soldier gets tangled up in things that distract him." Paul knew a soldier was to be first and foremost a soldier—in heart, soul, and mind. He was to live, eat, and breathe being a soldier. It is the same for believers.

Paul also knew soldiers were trained in obedience to their commanders. They did what they were supposed to do without necessarily knowing all the reasons. They trusted in their commander who saw the big picture and knew the reasons.

The soldier, athlete, and farmer all work for something that is in the future: the soldier, for the hope of victory; the athlete, for the hope of winning the prize; the farmer, for the coming harvest. What the believer works toward is also in the future. It is to hear God's words, "Well done, good and faithful servant."

Soldiers were also willing to suffer and to sacrifice for their ruler's cause. They remained loyal and faithful even in the face of death. This is a picture of how the believer should be who serves not a commander of an army, but the God who made the universe.

Paul continued with another picture of a believer— an athlete—giving the example of one who trains hard. It is not an example of a person who does just enough to get by, but one who strives to compete according to the rules and standards of excellence.

Athletes are not lazy. They set a standard for themselves and then train their bodies accordingly. The believer should do the same. He should not lower his standards, but rather live his life within them, ever striving for excellence.

Paul's last example was that of a farmer. The farmer knows there are no quick results. After planting and working, the farmer has to patiently wait for the rewards. The farmer's work is never done. This is how the believer is to be—always at his job of being a Christian.

"Believers are to follow the example of the soldier, athlete, and farmer," Paul instructed. "They must not get distracted by useless arguments, empty talk, or trying to win the approval of others. Instead, they should be concerned about God's approval. Everyone who is a believer should stay away from evil and live their lives in such a way that they are always available to be used by God. Much like a vessel that is kept clean so it can be used, believers are to be full of honor, set apart, and useful to the Master. They are to be like workers who are not a cause for shame."

CLIMBING ONWARD

Look up II Timothy 2:15. What does it say? What are two descriptions of a person who is approved of by God?

Skill Time

Handling the Word of God correctly means spending time in it and knowing your way around its contents. The results are a changed life and a good example of a believer. Have you been faithful to look up all the verses in CLIMBING ONWARD or just those you were most interested in, or couldn't guess? Stop now and take this time to go back and answer any you may have skipped or neglected. Then, commit in your heart to know God's Word.

THIS IS GETTING UGLY

TAKEN FROM II TIMOTHY 3

GETTING READY

Spend a few minutes thinking about God's comfort and help. Thank Him that He is always near and ready to help you weather any storm—no matter how ugly it gets.

THE JOURNEY

Do you ever feel that you're purposefully picked on or hurt because you're a Christian?

Paul knew first-hand what persecution was like. In his lifetime he had been in the center of riots, falsely accused, beaten, driven out of cities, imprisoned, threatened, stoned, and even left for dead! He had been treated as a hero and then sentenced as a criminal. Paul faced a lot of suffering, but it didn't stop him from loving his Lord or serving Him. As Paul faced death, his heart went out to Timothy. Paul wanted Timothy to continue to stand strong in his faith even in the difficult times to come.

Paul wrote, "Realize that in the last days, there will be difficult times. Men will seek after their own desires rather than seeking after God. They will be lovers of self who do things only to make themselves feel good. They will love money and wrap their lives around things money can buy. Men will talk better of themselves than they are deserving of and will make promises they can't keep. In their pride, they will stir up arguments and fights. They are people who are out of control: disobedient to their parents, ungrateful for what they have, disrespectful toward God, and unloving toward others. Because of this, they will be unforgiving of others and hold a grudge while freely gossiping and slandering others."

Paul knew Christians were a target for these people. "Don't be taken by surprise. These people will be cruel. They are unable to be trusted; they lie by saying one thing and then doing another. Their hearts are full of conceit. They laugh at others and live only for their own pleasures. Some may even hold to a form of godliness, but they deny its power. They may know about God, but they do not know Him. It won't be long before their wrong ways become known to all."

Paul described to Timothy some of his own sufferings at the hands of such people. "You yourself know of the sufferings I have experienced. You know what happened to me at Antioch, Iconium, and Lystra, and the persecutions I endured. You saw that in each and every one of them, the Lord delivered me!" The Lord did not keep Paul from experiencing persecutions. Instead, God faithfully helped Paul as he went through them.

"Know in advance that all who are determined to live a godly life will be persecuted," Paul warned. "For evil men go only from bad to worse. But don't be discouraged, Timothy. Instead, continue in your walk with the Lord and strive to live a godly life. Hold onto the Scriptures for they are able to give you the teaching, wisdom, and strength you need to live in this ungodly world and to face the challenges that will come your way."

CLIMBING ONWARD

Look up II Timothy 3:12. Why do you think this is so? Now turn back a few books to II Corinthians 12:9, 10 and read. (Go on, look it up! These are great verses!)

The next time you face persecution for being a Christian, will you be shocked, or will you be ready to stand?

CHECK IT OUT

TAKEN FROM II TIMOTHY 3—4

GETTING READY

Before you finish your walk through II Timothy, think about the part you allow Scripture to play in your life. Be honest. Ask God to forgive you for the times you leave His Word behind—unread, unheard, and unheeded.

THE JOURNEY

How would you answer the person who says, "The Bible is just an old, outdated book. It has nothing to say that would benefit me!"?

"Timothy," Paul charged, "hold onto the Scriptures for they are able to give you the teaching, wisdom, and strength you need to live in this ungodly world."

These were not words that Paul made up to make Timothy think highly of the Scriptures. They were something Paul had personally experienced, tested, tried, and knew to be true. The Scriptures are God's Words of comfort, encouragement, instruction, and correction. They are not man's words, but God's communication to people. The Scriptures are special, holy, dependable, and true because they come from God.

"All Scripture is God–breathed," Paul wrote, explaining how God put into the minds of godly men what to write. God carefully guided every thought so that the Scriptures became God's words to man—accurate and without mistake. "And it is useful," Paul explained. The Scriptures are words specially designed for us. These words are practical and purposeful. Since God made us, He knows us the best. His words are like an instruction book or owner's manual about our lives and how we operate the best.

Paul's next words describe the many things Scripture accomplishes in our lives. "It is useful for teaching, reproof, correction, and for training in righteousness." God's Word is useful for teaching us how to live God's way (teaching); if we get off the track, it is able to show us where we went wrong (reproof); it then points out how we can get back on track (correction). God's Word applies to how we live here and now. It is able to train us in righteousness so we can be equipped and ready for every good work.

> "God—breathed" is another way of saying inspired by God. It means that the words we have are His communication to us. They are true and accurate.

It has been said that God's Word, the Bible, is like His love letter to us. In it we see who we are and a glimpse of all that He is. We see our weakness and His strength, our problems and His solutions, our selfishness and His love, our faltering and His faithfulness. God's Word is not just a book written long ago; it is God's message to each of us—personally.

Read II Timothy 3:16, 17. Think about how you have seen this in your life.

Skill Time

The next time you hear a friend talking about the Bible as an outdated book of little or no value, what will you say? Take a few moments to think about what you know and have learned or have personally experienced concerning God's Word.

Now, on a piece of paper or a note card, finish the following statement: The Bible is not an outdated book of little or no benefit. I know because . . .

GETTING YOUR BEARINGS:
THE BOOK OF TITUS

Titus was a Gentile believer who served and traveled with the apostle Paul. Titus was dependable, willing, and able to do any task set before him. As a result, when Paul needed a trusted messenger to deliver a harsh letter to the troubled church in Corinth, he sent Titus.

After Paul's release from his first imprisonment in Rome, he took not only Timothy, but also Titus with him on his journey to revisit the churches. After leaving Timothy at Ephesus, Titus and Paul traveled to Crete where Titus stayed behind to help bring needed changes to the church there. The Book of Titus is Paul's letter of instruction to Titus, reminding him of what he is to teach the Cretan believers.

As you journey through Titus, notice the important thing Paul reminds Titus to teach. It is something their whole walk with God is built upon.

DON'T FORGET

TAKEN FROM TITUS 2—3

GETTING READY

As you journey through Titus, think about your life. Think about the things you did and thought before you became a Christian. (If you're not sure you are a Christian, turn to the back of this book and read the special message for you.) Ask God to remind you of what He has done in and through your life.

THE JOURNEY

How does it feel when you see pictures of yourself as a baby? Do the pictures bring back any memories?

Paul thought for a moment while his pen rested on the parchment. The churches in Crete were having trouble knowing what and in whom to believe. Titus had stayed behind, tending to this matter, yet Paul still felt heavy-hearted. He must write a letter of encouragement and instruction to Titus, telling him what to remind the believers of and what things to teach them.

"Tell the believers to pay no attention to the non-believing Jews who have rejected the truth. They claim to know God, but by their own actions, they deny Him. Challenge the believers not to listen to such men, but to stand firm in the truth," Paul wrote.

"Teach older men to live worthy of respect, to be self-controlled, and to show great love and faith. Likewise, older women should be respectful in the way they live, not slandering others with their words, but teaching what is good," Paul instructed. He continued, describing how young men, young women, and even slaves were to act as believers. "For God's grace, which brings salvation to all men, teaches us to say no to ungodliness. It teaches us to live self-controlled and godly lives while we are here on earth. We are to live such lives while we wait for Jesus Christ to come back again in all His glory!"

Paul paused a moment, thinking back on what they were like before they gave their lives to following Jesus. "At one time, we were foolish, laughing at the thought of someone dying on a cross for our sins. We thought we were smart, when really we were deceived, not knowing the truth. We thought we were free, when we were actually slaves to our own uncontrollable desires. We constantly lived in anger and were envious of others, not wanting them to have good things or success. We secretly hated others and were being hated in return.

Crete is a mountainous island located southeast of Greece. It was a place Paul had never visited while on his missionary journeys. Where did these believers come from? It is believed they were travelers who journeyed into Jerusalem during the time of Pentecost and who returned home to Crete as Christians.

"But, in the midst of this, God came and did something about it. In His great kindness and love, He saved us from our own sins, not because of righteous things we had done, but because of His mercy. Not only did He save us, but He gave us His Holy Spirit so we would have the power and ability to live godly lives.

"Titus, teach the believers to devote themselves to doing what is good. Teach them to live, worthy of God by reminding them of all God has done for them. Remind them of their past, so they will continue to live for God in the future."

CLIMBING ONWARD

Read Titus 2:14. What were the two results of Jesus giving Himself for our sins? How should we then live?

Skill Time

Sometimes it's good to look back and remember what you were like before you were saved by Jesus. Remembering helps you become more thankful for all He has and is doing for you.

Take a piece of paper and draw a line down the middle. On the left hand side, draw a big circle. In that circle, write words that describe what you were like before you came to know Jesus. (Draw pictures if you prefer.) Now, on the right hand side, draw a big circle. In this circle, write or draw descriptions of what God is helping you to become.

Read Titus 3:3-5. Under the left hand circle, write Titus 3:3. Under the right hand circle, write Titus 3:4-5. Now, draw a big line through the circle on the left. It is because of God's work in your life that you no longer have to live like that. Take a few minutes to thank God, and tell Jesus that you love and appreciate Him.

GETTING YOUR BEARINGS:
THE BOOK OF PHILEMON

The Book of Philemon was written during Paul's first imprisonment in Rome, around the same time he wrote Colossians. This prison letter is a personal letter addressed to a man named Philemon who lived in the city of Colosse.

Philemon was a wealthy Christian in whose home the church met. He had become a believer through Paul's ministry. Apparently Philemon had slaves (as did all wealthy people), and one slave, named Onesimus, stole from Philemon and ran off to Rome to become lost in the crowds.

While in Rome, Onesimus met Paul and became a believer in Christ. Even though he had become very helpful to Paul, Paul knew Onesimus must make right the wrongs he had done. As a result, Paul sent Onesimus back to Philemon with a letter in hand, asking Philemon to forgive and accept Onesimus back.

As you journey through the short Book of Philemon, notice the theme of forgiveness. Notice, too, how Paul (who had done no wrong) offers to pay for Onesimus's debts (what Onesimus owed because of the wrong he did). Paul's offer is a great example of the Gospel and what Jesus did for us.

WILL YOU?

TAKEN FROM PHILEMON 1

GETTING READY

Pray, asking God to speak to your heart. Ask Him to show you anyone you might need to forgive.

THE JOURNEY

Is asking for forgiveness and forgiving others sometimes difficult for you to do?

As Onesimus walked, he clutched Paul's letter tightly in his hands. His heart pounded as he wondered how Philemon would respond. Yes, he had done something terribly wrong against his master, Philemon—he had stolen from him and had run away. Although slaves were often treated as mere property, Onesimus had never been mistreated by Philemon. Yet, Onesimus didn't think twice about what he was doing at the time; he just wanted his freedom. That was then, this was now.

Now, Onesimus was experiencing freedom, but of a much different kind! Never had Onesimus known such peace! Although physically he was a slave, he was no longer a slave spiritually! He now served a new Master—the Lord Jesus Christ.

Onesimus continued to walk, not knowing what lay before him. He carried a letter from Paul, asking Philemon to forgive and accept him back, not just as a slave, but as a brother in Christ. "I ask you on the basis of love," Paul wrote, "that you do what is right. I am writing concerning your slave Onesimus. Before this slave was useless to you, but now he has become useful in a new way," Paul explained. The name Onesimus was a common name for slaves and it meant useful.

There were sixty million slaves in the Roman Empire during the time this letter was written. Due to fear of such a large number causing possible trouble, soldiers kept a watchful eye to maintain order. Rebellious slaves were not tolerated. When Paul sent Onesimus back to Philemon, he was taking a great risk. When Onesimus went back, he was taking a great step of faith.

Having become a believer, Onesimus was very helpful to Paul while he was imprisoned. He was such a great help, Paul almost wished to keep Onesimus rather than send him back. "He is very dear to me," Paul wrote, "welcome him back as a brother in the Lord. Welcome him as you would welcome me."

Paul knew this could be a difficult thing for Philemon. Rebellious slaves were usually put to death. Runaway slaves were branded on the forehead with a hot iron so all would know their disgrace. Paul was not only asking Philemon to accept Onesimus back, he was also asking Philemon to forgive the slave and to honor him as a brother in the Lord! Philemon would have no time to think it over. Onesimus would be right there, having delivered the letter in person. "If Onesimus has done you any wrong or owes you any money, I will personally pay it back," Paul offered. He knew he could trust Onesimus, and he knew he could expect Philemon to do what was right in God's sight.

Onesimus clutched the parchment in his hands as he neared Philemon's house, wondering what Philemon's response would be.

CLIMBING ONWARD

Turn to Philemon 7. (Since Philemon is only one chapter long, the 7 stands for the verse number.) Look at the description of Philemon toward the end of the verse. What does this tell you about Philemon? Do you think he was one to forgive or one to hold a grudge?

> The name Philemon meant *loving*, apparently it was a very fitting name!

Tradition has it that Philemon not only forgave Onesimus, but granted his freedom so he might return to Paul and help out in the ministry. It has been recorded that fifty years after this incident there was a church leader in Ephesus named Onesimus. Could it be the same one? It very well could!

THINKING on your FEET

When a person who has wronged you in a hurtful way comes back to ask for forgiveness, how will you respond?

GETTING YOUR BEARINGS:
THE BOOK OF HEBREWS

Hebrews is a fantastic book because it allows us to see what Jesus is doing for us today! Unlike the other New Testament books, we're really not sure who wrote the book. Some have suggested Paul wrote it, while others suggest a coworker such as Barnabas or Apollos. We don't know exactly who it was written to, although we know it was written to Jewish believers before A.D. 70. The important thing about the Book of Hebrews is not who wrote it or when it was written. The important thing is that God wanted it to be part of the Scriptures. He has a special message for us in this book.

As you journey through Hebrews, note that it was written to believing Jews who were in danger of going back to their old Jewish religion, turning their backs on Christ. A phrase that repeats itself throughout this book is "consider Jesus, our great High Priest." Apparently there were things causing the believers to drift away from their relationship with Jesus. They needed to be brought back to seeing Jesus for who He is and to remembering all He does for them.

HE KNOWS

TAKEN FROM HEBREWS 4

GETTING READY

Think about your relationship with Jesus. Is it what it should be? Talk to Jesus about it and ask Him to help you grow closer to Him.

THE JOURNEY

Have you ever told only part of the truth about something because you were afraid if you told the whole truth you'd get in trouble?

No doubt about it—the Jewish believers were drifting from the Lord. Some were interested in angels, others in keeping the laws and going back to meaningless ceremonies. "Pay careful attention to the Gospel you heard so you don't drift away!" the writer to the Hebrews warned. "In the past God spoke through the prophets and the Old Testament Scriptures, but now He has spoken to us through His Son!"

The writer explained how everything in the Old Testament points to Jesus. He also explained how Jesus is greater than anything or anyone—including Moses who gave them the laws! "Make sure you don't drift away from the living God by having hearts that turn away from Him in unbelief and sin." He quoted Psalm 95—something with which they were very familiar. It talks of Israel's turning from God, and the results of it!

"No one can hide or try to keep anything from God, for nothing is hidden from His sight," the writer warned. "Everything is uncovered and naked before Him." The words the writer used were ones the believers understood. The words "nothing hidden from His sight" were used of wrestling. It described when the opponent grabbed a person by the throat so he could not move or escape. Instead, he had to gaze into the face of his opponent. It was also used for skinning animals. The outside skin would be stripped away, and all that would be left was what the animal was like underneath. Lastly, they were the same words used for criminals who had a dagger placed under their chin when on trial. This dagger kept them from bowing their head and hiding their face. So it is with believers. Nothing is hidden from God's sight. God can see past the outside things we see. God looks straight into the heart; He cannot be fooled. Israel's sin in the past was not only in turning their hearts from God, but also in thinking God didn't know any better!

Two-edged swords were very sharp (like a razor) and very exact. They were able to cut through the most difficult things with great ease.

The writer went on to explain how God's Word helps to uncover things believers try to cover up or deny. "For God's Word is sharper than any two-edged sword! It is living and active; able to cut through false-hoods and get at the heart of things. God's Word can judge the thoughts and the attitudes of the heart."

CLIMBING ONWARD

Look up Hebrews 4:13. What does this verse tell you about God? Who do we really have to answer to? Is He fooled? Read verse 16. Knowing that God knows everything, this is how we should openly respond to Him.

DANGER AHEAD

When you mess up, you will be tempted to try to hide from God. Don't. He already knows what you have done and all the thoughts that have gone through your mind. You can never tell Him half the truth—He knows the whole story. Don't run from God. Instead, run to Him. He wants you to draw near to Him so that He may help you. His mercy and grace are yours for the asking. Nothing can make Him love you more than He does, and nothing can make Him love you less. Never forget that.

BUT WHY?

TAKEN FROM HEBREWS 4—10

GETTING READY

Stop and pray. Ask God to help you understand and appreciate all it cost Him to offer you forgiveness.

THE JOURNEY

Jesus died for our sins, but have you ever won— wondered why?

The writer of Hebrews answers this question for us by comparing Jesus to a high priest. The main theme of Hebrews is consider Jesus, our great High Priest. But, just what is a high priest, and what does he do?

In the Old and New Testament, the high priest acted as a bridge between man and God. On the Day of Atonement once a year, the high priest went into the holy of holies in the temple to make a sin sacrifice for all the people. This was done with great fear and only after the high priest had completed several ceremonies to cleanse his own sin. The high priest made his sacrificial offering for the people, then left the presence of God as quickly as possible. Why did the high priest have to make a sacrifice for sin?

Long ago, when God made Adam and Eve, He gave certain rules for their relationship with Him. When the rules were broken, sin entered the picture and Adam and Eve could no longer keep their same relationship with God. As a result, they hid from God and tried to cover their sin. (Big mistake!) God forgave them, but the consequences of sin remained. Blood had to be shed to cover their sin—thus, the first sacrifice.

In both Old and New Testament times, blood was thought of as life itself. Today, we know that blood cleans our wounds and carries the necessary ingredients to help our bodies heal. People in Bible times knew blood was not cheap, but cost dearly; something had to die in order for blood to be available as a sacrifice. Sacrifices were an ongoing thing because people continually sinned. The sacrifices the high priest offered were only temporary. They were not a permanent nor perfect solution.

In Hebrews 10:22 *sprinkled* refers to blood that was sprinkled on things to make them holy and sinless. Washing with pure water was something the high priest did before he offered the sacrifices.

The writer of Hebrews showed them how the law and the sacrifices were unable to deal with the cause of sin. At best, they just showed man's sin all the more and his need of a Savior. This was where he introduced Jesus as the great High Priest.

High priests eventually died, but Jesus is a priest who lives forever! High priests had to offer sacrifices for their own sins. Jesus the High Priest is sinless and has no need to offer sacrifices for Himself. High priests had to continually offer sacrifices—the job was never done. Jesus the High Priest offered Himself as a sacrifice—once for all—then sat in glory in heaven. High priests passed through the curtain in the Temple to enter the holy of holies once a year, offering their sacrifices. Jesus passed through the heavens from the very throne of God and gave Himself as a sacrifice. Then He returned to the heavenly holy of holies where He sat in glory. Jesus was more than a bridge between man and God, He was the key that opened the door permanently so that any person can actually go into the very presence of God!

Jesus was the perfect High Priest and the perfect sacrifice! When He offered up His life, Jesus made it possible for people to be forgiven and to live a godly life in the future! Unlike animals that were sacrificed against their will, Jesus voluntarily gave His life. The animals were sacrificed because of law; Jesus gave Himself as a sacrifice out of love. The animal didn't know what was happening; Jesus knew what He was doing. He was not a victim but did what He did, fully knowing all that it would cost Him.

Because of Jesus' sacrifice, our hearts can be washed clean and our lives freed from sin. Because of Jesus acting as our High Priest, we can draw near to God and have the privilege of knowing Him as our heavenly Father.

The holy of holies in the temple was only a type, or model, of what the throne of God is like in heaven. After Jesus offered Himself as a sacrifice, He went back to the (real) holy of holies and paved the way for us to follow.

CLIMBING ONWARD

Find Hebrews 10:10 and read it. Through Jesus we have been made holy in God's sight once for all. Now, skip down to verse 19 and then 22-24. What does it say? Since we have this ability to stand before God, what should be our response? (See the first part of verse 22, first part of verse 23, and verse 24).

Skill Time

God wants us to draw near to Him with full assurance. It was at great cost that He opened a way for us to be able to come before His holy presence. Do you appreciate the opportunity you have? Think about the time you spend in prayer. Do you hand God your wish list of prayer requests, or do you take time to worship and really talk to Him? Spend a few minutes right, now thanking Him for what He has provided and worshiping Him for who He is!

Sign Me Up

TAKEN FROM HEBREWS 11

Getting Ready

Ask God to speak to your heart so you might clearly understand His Word. Ask Him to challenge you and help you in areas where your faith is weak.

The Journey

How do you know as a Christian that your faith is the right one?

Not all faith is the right kind of faith. The value of your faith is only as good as the thing in which you have put your faith. A good definition of the right kind of faith is "believing and trusting in God's character." That means believing that God is who He says He is, and that He will do what He says He will do.

"Faith is being sure of what we have put our hope in (God) and being certain of what we do not see (the promises of God yet to be fulfilled). This type of faith is what some of our forefathers were praised for," the writer of Hebrews wrote as he listed great heroes of faith.

"By faith, Abel's offering was accepted by God. By faith, Noah listened to God's warnings and obediently built an ark even though there was no sign of rain. By faith, Abraham became a father—even when he was too old to have children—because God made a promise to him and Abraham believed. By faith, God's people crossed through the Red Sea on dry land, while the Egyptians were drowned, and by faith the walls of Jericho came crashing down. All these people were able to experience great things in their lives because they knew and believed in the living God. Their faith was in the right One."

The writer of Hebrews continued by providing more examples of those who had placed their trust in God and were not disappointed. "I have not even mentioned Gideon, Samson, David, Samuel, or any of the prophets! Through their faith, they conquered kingdoms, received what God promised, shut the mouths of lions, survived the fiery furnace, had their weaknesses turned into strengths, and became powerful in battle! Still other believers were tortured and killed for their faith. Some faced jeers and flogging, while others were thrown in prison in chains. They were stoned, sawed in two, and put to death by the sword. Some had opportunity to be released, but they refused to deny their Lord. They knew in whom they believed, and they were willing to die before they would ever turn from their God."

> Hebrews 11 has often been referred to as "the believers' hall of fame." It shows ordinary people who became heroes through their obedience and faith in God and God alone.

The words the writer of Hebrews wrote were powerful. His readers would know immediately the full stories behind the names he mentioned. They would see the great examples of the right kind of faith and understand even better that God was and is the only true God. As a result, they would be encouraged in their faith. Perhaps even one day, their own names would be added to the list of those who have found God to be all that He says He is.

CLIMBING ONWARD

What you put your faith in is very important. In your Bible, turn to Hebrews 11:6. What two things do people who come to God need to believe? What pleases God?

DANGER AHEAD

Everyone has faith in something. Those who don't believe in God have faith in themselves or a god they have created in their own mind (big mistake!). They will make excuses, saying, "Christianity is a blind faith." Such people are wrong and only kidding themselves.

The changed lives of people who have gone before you are just one proof that God is real and His ways are right. Stand confident in this. Look to God and know He will reward your faith. Keep your eyes on Him and live for Him. Follow the example of the great heroes of faith who have gone before you.

I THINK I CAN

TAKEN FROM HEBREWS 12

GETTING READY

Take a few minutes to talk with God. Thank Him for those who have gone before you and have set an example of what it is like to follow after God with a whole heart. Ask God to make you like that as well.

THE JOURNEY

How often do you start something, but run out of steam before finishing?

Boredom. Distractions. Wanting rewards and results *now*. Busyness with other things. . . . These all keep people from finishing what they start. Little by little these things begin to destroy people's desire to stick with what they are doing. Little by little these things pull people away from their goal.

The writer of Hebrews was aware of this and knew it was something all believers face. Having already challenged the believers to follow in the steps of many strong Christians who had gone before them, he now explained why and how it is done. Such strong faith is possible and its rewards are far greater than anything imaginable! Having directed their eyes to the example of others, the writer now directed their eyes to their own personal walk with God. Believers are not to become lazy, thinking everything will work out in the end. Instead, they must see the goal and keep running toward it, much like an athlete runs in a race.

"Let us throw off everything that keeps us from running well," It was unheard of for an Olympic runner to race with a backpack and his arms full of things he is interested in! It was a commonly known fact that an Olympic runner couldn't run well if he was carrying extra weight, so he threw off everything and ran with only the necessary things. The writer of Hebrews stated, "Let us get rid of the sin that so easily entangles us." *Entangle* means having something fall down around one's feet, tripping one up (which is exactly what sin does!). A runner usually prepared by removing any unnecessary clothes. As believers, we need to take off the sin we often allow ourselves to wear, not thinking it will cause any harm.

The Greek word used in the Bible for "growing weary" (fainting) is the same word used to describe how an athlete throws himself onto the ground and collapses after crossing the finish line. We are challenged not to give up until we cross the finish line.

The writer continued, "After we have done this, let us run with determination the race that is set before us. Let us fix our eyes on becoming more like Jesus. He is both the author and the one who helps us in our faith. " The writer knew that as believers, we shouldn't be strolling along in our walk with God; we are to be heading towards our goal—the goal of becoming more like Jesus. We are to be as pilgrims, forever traveling onward.

"Consider Jesus and all that He has done; for Jesus was willing to give up His privileges as God and to be beaten, misunderstood, and to die on the cross for you. He made it possible for you to have a relationship with God. Do not grow weary or lose heart, but keep your focus on Him and run the race to the finish!"

Find Hebrews 12:2. What three things does this tell us about Jesus? Upon what should our eyes be fixed? Jesus will help us run well for Him. He has already seen the track and understands the difficulties and uphill climbs.

CROSS ROADS

What type of runner will you be: one who is focused on the goal and wins, or one who gets tangled up, runs out of steam, and is defeated? What makes the difference?

IT'S MY CHOICE

TAKEN FROM HEBREWS 13

GETTING READY

As you finish your journey through the Book of Hebrews, think about your life and where you stand. Are you satisfied? Spend a few minutes talking to God about it.

THE JOURNEY

Have you ever been unsatisfied in your life, where nothing you had or did seemed to please you?

Like using a remote control on a VCR, the writer of Hebrews did a quick rewind to review what Jesus did in the past and still does for believers. Then he allowed us to see real examples of common people in the past who stood strong in the faith. With a quick touch of the fast forward button he challenged us to keep our eyes on the goal set before us. Now, it's as if he has hit the play button, and has brought us to the present time—where we are now in our walk with the Lord. The author gave practical instructions, challenges, warnings, and encouragement before closing his letter.

"Keep loving each other and remember those who are suffering and in prison," he wrote to the believers. The degree to which they did this would show the depth of their walk with the Lord. "Keep yourselves pure and keep your lives free from the love of money. Do not be greedy, but be satisfied and content with what you have." The writer knew how important it was that they keep first things first and not seek after things that don't last or can't satisfy. "Even if you have very little, you still have the Lord and His help, for God Himself has said, 'Never will I leave you; never will I turn my back on you.'"

> "Never will I leave you" and "the Lord is my helper" were quotes from two Old Testament passages: Joshua 1:5 and Psalm 118:7. They show that believers need nothing more because they have the help and the presence of God in their lives. Nothing is greater than that!

The writer knew these were important words for there would be times in their lives when they would face the temptation of being dissatisfied would be strong. Believers might compare themselves to others and begin feeling discontent. Perhaps they would even turn to other people or things to meet their needs. The author showed believers they need nothing more, for they have the very presence and help of God in their lives. Nothing man has to offer could bring greater satisfaction! "Because of this, we can boldly say, 'The Lord is my helper; I will not be afraid'." Believers need not worry, for nothing man can do will take away what they have in God.

"Remember those who have gone before you as examples in the faith, and how the Lord met their every need. Jesus is the same yesterday, as He is today, and will be tomorrow! Let us continually offer praise to God through and because of Jesus."

Look up Hebrews 13:8. What does this tell you about Jesus? Everything you've learned about Jesus so far was true in the past, is true today, and will continue to be true. Jesus is trustworthy. He has proven Himself. He can meet your needs.

THINKING on your FEET

If you could choose anyone or anything to meet your needs and build your life upon, who or what would you choose? Why?

Getting Your Bearings:
THE BOOK OF JAMES

James is a dynamite book packed with very practical words on how to live. Some have called it the "Proverbs of the New Testament" because it is so rich in advice! The Book of James was written by Jesus' half brother (named James) and is thought to be the first of the New Testament books to be written.

The fact that James wrote this book is very special, for James and his brothers (Joses, Simon, and Jude) did not believe in Jesus as Savior and Lord while Jesus was living among them. It wasn't until after Jesus rose from the dead that James became a believer (Acts 1:14). It is also interesting to note that James grew into Peter's position as leader of the church in Jerusalem (Acts 12:17).

James wrote this book as a letter to Jewish believers who were scattered. As you journey through James, watch where you step and how you walk, for the book of James stands as a challenge to the way you live—in your actions (or lack of them), in your speech, and in your conduct toward others.

JUST DO IT

TAKEN FROM JAMES 1

GETTING READY

Ask the Lord to speak to your heart and help you be a doer of His Word.

THE JOURNEY

Do you ever see kids at school trying to act like someone else?

In order to be like someone else, people do what the person they want to be like does. They study that person and imitate his actions. They try to talk like her. They are constantly checking out the other person so they can remember how that person acts. Even though they are imitating the wrong thing, their actions are a good practice!

Believe it or not, James is writing to the Jewish Christians about doing this very thing! They are to observe the Scriptures, then act upon what they know and allow it to change their behavior.

James wrote, "Don't just hear God's Word, thinking that is all that is necessary. For such thinking is wrong, and those who think this way are deceiving themselves. Instead, pay close attention to God's Word and then become a doer of it. Examine it. Study it. Put it into practice."

James knew it wasn't good enough just to know about God's Word; knowing about something never changed a life. Instead, believers needed to act upon what they knew. "Anyone who just hears the Word but doesn't do what it says is like a man who looks at himself in a mirror. He sees things about himself that need to be fixed, but instead of doing something about it, he simply walks away. The result is that he has forgotten what he looked like and the things that needed to be changed. Even though he looked in the mirror, it really made no difference in his life."

"However, the man who gives his attention to looking into God's Word and acting upon what he sees, this man will be blessed," James wrote. "Be like this man. Be doers of the Word, not just hearers only," he warned.

> A "*doer*" isn't someone who tries to tackle being perfect. It is someone who takes little steps of obedience and lets God tackle the rest.

James's warning carries a strong message to us. While some people are busy trying to act like somebody they're not, some Christians forget to act like the somebody they are! They do this because they aren't checking out God's Word and putting it into action. As for practical advice when it comes to God's Word, there are only three words to remember—just do it.

CLIMBING ONWARD

Read James 1:25. What is the promise for those who strive to put God's Word into practice in their lives?

Skill Time

Have you learned or personally read something in the Scriptures that really challenged you? Something you know you need to do (or stop doing)? What is it? Have you done anything about it?

Often we don't act upon something because we don't have a game plan or because we don't commit in our hearts to do it. What is God tugging at your heart about? Write it down on a piece of scrap paper.

Ask forgiveness for not dealing with what you wrote down. Then, commit it to God. Tell Him you want to do something about it and need His help. Then, the next time this area comes up, demonstrate your sincerity by acting upon that which you know to do. God will be right there to help you.

DID I SAY THAT?

TAKEN FROM JAMES 3

GETTING READY

Take a few minutes and think about things that have been said to your face or about you behind your back. If this brings up bad feelings, take them to God. Ask God to heal your hurt feelings and help you not to use your tongue as a weapon.

THE JOURNEY

Do you know kids who tend to put other people down with their words?

James thought for a moment as his pen rested on the parchment. Words are powerful things. They are used to build people up or to tear them down. The way people use their words often shows where their heart is. For believers, our choice of words and the use of our tongue should be to build up others and glorify the Lord. Such was not the case with the believers to whom James was writing. In his letter, he wrote to challenge them.

"We all stumble in many ways, and perhaps the greatest way we all stumble is in the use of our tongue," James wrote. "This is an area where we all need work. The tongue is very powerful even though it is small. A large horse is controlled and directed by a bit placed in its mouth. Large ships, even though driven by strong winds, are steered by a small rudder. Such small things as a bit or a rudder have power to change the course and direction of a horse or ship! So it is with a person's tongue. It is small, but it can easily lead him in places he doesn't desire to go."

James continued, "The tongue is such a small part of the body, yet it makes great boasts and gets us into trouble! Think about how a whole forest is set on fire because of one spark! In like manner, the tongue is capable of setting fire to the course of a person's life. It ends up destroying everything in its path—including the things that were good.

"It is with our tongue that we bless the Lord and with that same tongue we talk down about others who are made in God's image. This should not be so!" James corrected. "Can fresh water and bitter water come from the same spring? No! Why then, do sweet words come out of the same mouth as bitter words? Can a grapevine bear olives? No! It doesn't make sense. So, words that destroy others are not fitting for the believer," James instructed.

> Whenever a Jewish person heard the name of God being mentioned, he was required to stop and say, "Blessed be He!" From this phrase we have "with our tongues we bless the Lord."

He explained how the believer's words were to be chosen and used with wisdom—wisdom that was from God and was pure, peace–loving, thoughtful of others, honoring, forgiving, and sincere.

Such control over the tongue and such wisdom is not something that comes naturally, but rather something people can do only with God's help. "Even though man can tame the wildest of animals, he cannot tame his own tongue by his own efforts," James wrote. Such things need the strength and help only God can provide.

CLIMBING ONWARD

Find James 3:9, 10. What does God have to say about the way we use our tongue?

Skill Time

Look up Proverbs 15:28 and underline it in your Bible. (This would be a good verse to memorize so you can always have it as a reminder!)

The next time you are tempted to open your mouth and say something, stop and ask yourself, "What would Jesus say in this situation?"

ME? ANGRY?

TAKEN FROM JAMES 4

GETTING READY

Think about what makes you angry and how you respond. Ask God to help you with this area of your life.

THE JOURNEY

Do you have a hard time controlling anger?

Have you ever felt so much frustration and anger that you just want to scream? Most of us have felt that way. Anger is a fact of life. But, why do we get angry? What causes it?

James had already written about the difference between hearing God's Word and obeying it by putting it into practice. James also wrote about the problem we all face with our tongue. Now James dove into another problem—the one called anger—and what causes it.

"What causes fights and quarrels among you?" James wrote. "It is your selfish desires that battle within you. You become angry because you desire to get something or have something happen that doesn't happen."

James knew this was the root cause of anger, but he also knew this was only the tip of the iceburg. "You get angry because you do not have something you want, and you do not have what you want because you don't take it to God and ask Him," James wrote. It was far easier to fight for something, demanding one's rights, than it was to humble oneself and take his wants and needs to God.

"Sometimes you don't receive what you ask from God because you ask with wrong motives. You ask so that you might be able to spend what you get on your own pleasures," James wrote.

It is not unnatural to want to win an argument for the sake of pride or to have something special happen to you so others might notice. These are all things someone might want and become angry about if he or she didn't get them. These are all things that result from wrong

> **Anger produces:**
> A—actions that are wrong.
> N—Neglect of doing what is right.
> G—Grief.
> E—Energy spent in selfish ways.
> R—Relationships that are damaged.

motives. The natural temptation is to fight with words or anger in order to make something happen and to try to get what is selfishly desired. That's the danger with the anger trap.

Anger comes from unmet needs or wants that are not taken to God. Anger is man's reaction when not getting his own way. Anger is sin.

Check out James 4:1, 2. What does it say? What do our desires cause us to do? What should we start doing with our desires? (Look at the last two words in verse 2.)

Skill Time

Before you let off steam the next time, examine your heart and ask yourself, "Whose interest am I looking out for—mine, or others?"

GETTING YOUR BEARINGS:
THE BOOK OF I PETER

First Peter was written by the apostle Peter, who had been one of the Lord's disciples. We know about Peter from the Gospels. From the first twelve chapters of Acts, we learn that Peter became a strong and respected leader over the Jerusalem church. God did great things in and through Peter's life, just as Jesus had promised.

Because Peter identifies himself by his Greek name (Peter) instead of his Jewish name (Simon) in this letter, we know he is writing to Greeks. He is writing to Greek believers who were scattered throughout the northern regions of Asia Minor—northern Pontus, Galatia, Cappadocia, Asia, and Bithynia due to persecution.

Because Peter didn't know the Greek language very well, he had the help of Silas to translate his message and write it down for him (I Peter 5:12). As you may remember, Silas was Paul's coworker on his second missionary journey, and was chosen to help deliver the Jerusalem council decision to the first Gentile church in Antioch. Silas was also a Roman citizen. The reason Peter wrote this letter was to encourage the believers who were suffering under terrible trials.

In the past, Rome had acted kindly toward Christians. Roman soldiers even rescued Paul from angry Jews! This was because the Jewish
religion was accepted and permitted by the state. Christianity and
Judaism were closely tied. However, the farther they split apart, the more
noticeable the differences became. Christians were easy to spot, and
therefore became an easy target. The stage was set for the madman
emperor named Nero.

When Nero attempted to burn down Rome so he might build it back
up again, he faced great anger from its people. Seeing this, he looked for
someone else to blame and found the Christians an easy target. Nero
stirred up an outbreak of hatred against the Christians, and they were
soon hated by their own countrymen. As a result, cruel and illegal things
were done to Christians, with Nero leading the way! Nero had Christians
rolled in pitch. He then set them on fire and used them as torches to
light his gardens.

As you journey through I Peter, notice what Peter tells the believers
to do in the midst of all this. See how he tells them to stand strong, what
he tells them to stand strong in, and why.

LIFETIME GUARANTEE

TAKEN FROM 1 PETER 1—2

GETTING READY

Think about the things you treasure and how long they will be important to you. Will any of them last forever? Are they able to give you strength, direction, hope, and encouragement? Take a few minutes to thank God for His Word and how it will stand even when everything around you starts falling apart.

THE JOURNEY

If someone asked you why the Bible is special and different than the holy books of other religions, what three reasons would you state?

Peter knew the believers needed encouragement, and they needed it now! They needed to have their thoughts focused—not on their trials and sufferings, but on God and the blessing of salvation. Peter had important things to say, but he started his letter with praise.

"Praise be to God, the Father of our Lord Jesus Christ! In His loving mercy He allows us to have a living hope in Jesus and a reward that will never die or fade away! You, who are shielded by God's power through faith, have this reward in heaven. Remember the hope you have because of Jesus and rejoice, even though for now you are suffering various trials," Peter said.

Peter explained that their suffering was a test that would prove the strength and purity of their faith. Much like fire proves how pure gold is, their fiery trials would prove how pure and true their faith was. Peter continued, encouraging them to stand strong. "Therefore, be self-controlled in your thoughts and actions," he challenged. "Keep your mind and heart on the hope you have in Jesus and the grace He has given you. Don't return the evil that is done to you, but rather live a holy life, for God has said, 'Be holy, because I am holy'."

Next Peter reminds his readers how they were saved from their empty way of life and born again through the Word of God. "God's Word never becomes old or outdated. Even though it was written long ago, it applies to us here and now. It is living and will never die. Unlike grass that withers or flowers that fade away, God's Word will remain forever, for it is God's words, not man's."

Peter knew as the believers remembered this, they would be able to trust and stand on God's promises found in the Scriptures. The Scriptures were special—not just because they were God's Word, but also because they had been proven, tried, tested, and found to be true. People will come and go, much like the grass, but God's Word never changes.

"Knowing this," Peter challenged, "you should have a thirst and desire to know God's Word just like a baby who craves milk. God's Word helps you grow in your faith. You have already tasted and seen that the Lord is good. Continue to stand firm by trusting His Word and all that He has given you," Peter encouraged.

CLIMBING ONWARD

God's Word is much greater than anything ever written, including holy books from other religions. God's Word and God's Word only has been proven to be without fault.

Look up I Peter 1:24, 25. What does it say? Now, skip down to chapter 2, verse 2. What are we instructed to do? What will this do for us?

DANGER AHEAD

You will run into people who will try to prove the Bible is wrong or full of mistakes. Don't worry. Over the ages, no one has ever been able to do this, nor will they ever be able to. God's Word has stood, and will continue to stand against the arguments of the smartest people. God's Word, the Bible, is absolute truth. There is no other like it. You have God's lifetime guarantee on that—both for this life and the one to come!

NO COMMENT

TAKEN FROM 1 PETER 2

GETTING READY

Spend a few minutes thinking about how Jesus suffered before He died on the cross and how He handled His suffering. Then, praise God for what Jesus did for you and the example He set.

THE JOURNEY

Have you ever been picked on, made fun of, or blamed for something you didn't do?

Previously Peter had reminded the believers to stand firm on God's Word. Now he reminded them of Jesus' example. "Jesus suffered for you. While He was suffering, He provided an example so that you may know how to act when you are suffering," Peter wrote. Peter knew how Jesus lived each day—he was an eye witness to Jesus' life. He had seen the crowds press in on Jesus, everyone wanting something and hoping to be healed. He had heard the crowds cheer when Jesus entered a village. He had seen Jesus' love, kindness, patience, and wisdom. He had heard Jesus' teachings and knew Jesus personally lived the very things He taught. Peter had been there when Jesus did miracles and when the crowds sang

His praises. Peter also had been there when things seemed to take a turn for the worse.

Peter closed his eyes for a moment as the memories returned. He recalled the example Jesus set while He suffered for something He did not do. Peter remembered the look of love in Jesus' eyes as Jesus thought only of those He was suffering for and not His own circumstances. Jesus didn't claim His rights as God, but held His power under control—willingly. All of these things burned an image in Peter's mind.

"Jesus suffered for you and left an example of how you should follow in His steps," Peter wrote to the believers. "Jesus Himself did nothing wrong— He was perfect and had no sin. No deceit was in His mouth. He spoke truth. When others angrily hurled insults at Him, He did not insult back. When Jesus was suffering, He did not make any threats. Instead, He put His life in the hands of God the Father, knowing that God judges justly and it is He who has the last word!"

Hurl means to throw something with great force and violence. Those who were hurling insults at Jesus were doing it to hurt Him. There was no mistake; Jesus was their target.

Peter continued, "Jesus who once was cheered as a hero, suffered the insult of being put to death as an outcast. He did this to bear our sins so we might be set free from sin and be able to live in righteousness before God." Peter sat back and thought about how Jesus never took His eyes off the one He served. Because He was God Himself, fully deserving of worship and praise, He suffered greater insult than any of us could ever suffer. *And yet*, Peter thought, *love still controlled His every action and thought*. Jesus set an example for us to follow.

CLIMBING ONWARD

Read I Peter 2:23. Find three things Jesus did while He was suffering. Jesus knew judgment would come in the end, and He entrusted Himself to God. God will set the record straight at the appropriate time.

THINKING on your FEET

Knowing Jesus' example, how will you try to react when others pick on you, make fun of you, or wrongly blame you?

LET ME TELL YOU

TAKEN FROM I PETER 3—5

GETTING READY

Take some time to talk with God. Ask Him to quiet your thoughts so you can learn from Him.

THE JOURNEY

Have kids ever treated you as different because you claim to be a Christian or choose to go to church? How did you feel?

Peter knew that sooner or later the lives of the believers as they followed Jesus' example (even unto death) would change. As they observed this change, non–believers would ask questions. Sometimes the questions might be asked in anger or frustration. Other times, they would be asked with a spark of admiration and respect for the believers courage.

Peter wrote, "My friends, do not be surprised at the painful trials that come into your life. Instead, look at them as opportunities to tell others about Jesus. In your hearts, keep Christ as Lord. Never lose sight of Him and live for Him in every circumstance."

Peter continued, "When people see your example, they will ask you the reason you are so different. They will want to know the reason for your hope. Always be prepared to give an answer to everyone who asks. Live your life in such a manner that it will bring people to ask questions!" Peter challenged. "But, when they do ask," he cautioned, "answer with gentleness and respect. Tell them about the Lord and what He has done for you."

Peter continued, giving specific challenges about living for God. "When some see your life, they will think you are strange for not joining them in their activities. Some may even give you a hard time. Don't worry; they will have to answer to God for their own actions. Instead, be clear minded and self-controlled so you can pray. Love each other deeply—for love bears with the sins and wrongs of others. Use whatever gifts and abilities you have been given to serve others. Serve and live for God through the strength He provides, so that in all areas of your life God may be praised," Peter encouraged.

> As your life brings honor to God, those around you will take notice. No matter what type of notice they take, it will always provide opportunity for you to share your faith.

"If you are insulted because you are different and you suffer for the name of Christ, consider it a compliment. It is obvious that God's blessing is upon you, and others can see it as well."

With words of encouragement to stand strong and to cast all their cares upon the Lord, Peter closed out his letter to the believers. He knew they were suffering, but he knew they were in good hands. Their suffering was not pointless, but rather purposeful; and their God was ever present and powerful to help them.

CLIMBING ONWARD

Find I Peter 3:15. What does it say? According to this verse, what are you challenged to do?

Skill Time

Reread the first sentence of I Peter 3:15. How do you think this is accomplished? Our hearts are often referred to as the place where we feel emotion. In our hearts we feel fear, frustration, joy, and love. We often let our heart rule our head, and our head rules our actions. Not good!

First Peter 3:15 talks about setting apart Christ as Lord. Where?—in our heart! Take a few moments to think about how you respond to circumstances around you. If you tend to react from your emotions (gut response), then you haven't set apart Christ as Lord in your heart. And, chances are, your life isn't causing others to ask questions.

Take time to do some business with God. Tell Him you want Him to be Lord of your heart. Memorize I Peter 3:15, and use it as your daily goal. Write it on a note card cut out in the shape of a crown, and place it in the bathroom on the mirror as a daily reminder.

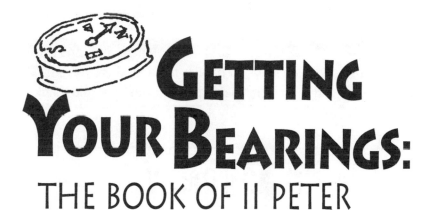

GETTING YOUR BEARINGS:
THE BOOK OF II PETER

Second Peter was written by Peter three years after his first letter. He wrote to the same group of believers, but the use of his Jewish name (Simon) indicates he was writing to others, too.

In his first letter, he warned and encouraged the believers about trials and sufferings from others. In this letter, Peter wrote to warn about the dangers from within. He challenged them to grow up in their faith and warned them to be careful about false teachings.

As Peter wrote this letter, he was in Rome facing certain death. Peter was killed by Nero in A.D. 67, around the same time Paul was killed. Peter's death was by crucifixion, and tradition has it that Peter asked to be crucified head downward. He felt unworthy to die as Jesus had.

MEASURE IT UP

TAKEN FROM II PETER 1

GETTING READY

Ask the Lord to show you where you stand spiritually. Ask Him to show you how you have grown and where you still need to grow. Ask Him to continue helping you in this area, and thank Him that He is a God who cares deeply for you.

THE JOURNEY

Have you ever wished there was a yardstick to measure spiritual growth and know how you were doing? Well, there is.

Peter knew he didn't have much longer to live. His heart yearned for the believers to whom he wrote. They needed to be challenged to grow spiritually so they could stand strong against false teachings.

"Through Jesus' divine power, we have been given everything we need to live life in a godly way. And this divine power comes through knowing and growing in our walk with Him," Peter wrote. This was the beginning point; faith in Jesus. This faith provides the foundation from which to start. Now, however, they needed to grow and mature in their faith by putting it into action and allowing it to change their lives.

Peter continued, "Through the help of the Holy Spirit, build upon the foundation of faith by practicing a life that shows goodness." The believers needed to act upon opportunities which God provided and to live the way God designed for them to live. This was the first step.

"Upon goodness," Peter wrote, describing the process of building with bricks, "add knowledge." This knowledge was a personal knowledge of God and something that would help them walk worthy of the Lord.

"Upon knowledge, add self-control," Peter challenged. It was one thing to be called to live a holy life and to get to know the Lord better, but it was another to let that knowledge change your actions and attitudes. Self-control is the determination to do what Jesus would do. This brought Peter to his next building block.

"Perseverance should be added to your self-control," he wrote. Perseverance is the continuing on to do what is right when your old sinful nature is trying to convince you to stop. Perseverance always keeps trying to do what it sets out to accomplish.

"Upon perseverance, add godliness," Peter continued. Godliness is of benefit for this life, as well in heaven. "Upon godliness, add brotherly kindness," Peter challenged. He knew being kind, tenderhearted, and forgiving of others as Christ forgave them would be a good measure of their spiritual growth.

Peter added, "Upon brotherly kindness, build love." Love was the highest achievement of all. For walking in love meant they had to be imitators of God. They would only be able to walk in God's kind of love as they started out their relationship with Him in faith, then grew in goodness, knowledge, self-control, perseverance, and godliness. As godliness was demonstrated in their lives they would be able to express kindness toward their brothers, and finally love toward all people—regardless. These were the building blocks to help measure their growth in the Lord.

Peter knew if the believers were to grow in these areas and mature in their personal walk with God, they would be able to stand strong—not only in the midst of their trials, but also against false teachings.

CLIMBING ONWARD

Look up II Peter 1:3. What does it say? Who gives us the strength to grow? Remember that it is the Holy Spirit who is battling in us to accomplish spiritual maturity. We must cooperate with Him by showing self-control and by never giving up the fight.

CROSS ROADS

Spiritually, are you growing or are you back at square one? Where have you grown? Where do you still need to grow?

SOMETHING'S WRONG HERE

GETTING READY

Thank the Lord that His Word is truth. Thank Him for the Holy Spirit who guides you in the ways of truth. Ask the Lord to protect you from false teachers who teach wrong things about God.

THE JOURNEY

Do you know how to identify false teachers?

Peter knew as the believers matured in their faith, they would be able to spot false teachers and wrong teachings. In the meantime, however, believers needed to be warned that such people existed. Some were even in the church, acting and pretending like they were believers!

"There are false teachers who are secretly introducing wrong teachings. They lay their wrong teachings next to the truth so people might consider them. Be careful! These false teachers are not always easy to spot, for they wrap their wrong teachings in just enough truth to make them seem all right at first glance," Peter warned. "Many people will be unknowingly led astray by these people."

Peter continued, "These people are controlled by their own desires and greed. Their words seem smooth and even desirable, yet they lead people further from the Lord." Peter knew that some people would dare to mock God saying, "Jesus isn't coming back! He promised to return, but just look how long it's been!" These false teachers purposefully stir up doubt in the Scriptures and the promises of God. They themselves are untaught and don't know the real truth.

The Greek word *false* is the same word from which we get the word *plastic*. The false teachers took their teachings and molded them (like plastic is molded) to fit people's circumstances, hoping to attract them.

Peter paused for a moment before closing his letter. He knew the seriousness of the matter and knew his warning would be well heeded. "Now that you have been warned about such people in advance," Peter wrote, "be on your guard so you are not carried away by their false teachings. Rather, concentrate your efforts on growing in the grace and knowledge of our Lord and Savior Jesus Christ. Grow in your walk with Him, and you will not fall into their traps."

CLIMBING ONWARD

Look up II Peter 3:17, 18. How are you to protect yourself from such false teachers?

DANGER AHEAD

There are many false teachers and religions who use Christian words but attach a different meaning to them. (The New Age movement is one such religion). Don't be fooled. Be on your guard, and continue to grow in your walk with the Lord. People who work in banks are able to spot counterfeit (false) money not because they study the different counterfeits, but because they study and are very familiar with the real thing. Those who are intimately acquainted with truth are those who can easily spot what is false.

GETTING YOUR BEARINGS:
THE BOOKS OF I, II, III JOHN

The books of I, II, and III John were written by the apostle John, who was the closest of all the disciples to Jesus. He was believed to have been born in the city of Bethsaida, the same hometown as Philip, Andrew, and Peter. John is also the author of the Gospel of John and of Revelation.

Although John didn't say to whom he was writing, it is commonly thought that he was addressing believers in Ephesus where he spent the last years of his life. For our journey through the New Testament, we will study only I John. You might want to read II and III John on your own—they contain some great treasures.

The purpose of I John is to give assurance to all believers. It seemed some believers were fighting with each other while others were quietly doubting their own salvation. With love and tenderness, John wrote to encourage them and set the record straight.

As you journey through I John take your time. Notice the great sense of encouragement you gain as you travel through this book.

TESTING 1, 2, 3

TAKEN FROM I JOHN 1—3

GETTING READY

Take time to prepare your heart just as you have been doing throughout this devotional. Get real before God by coming honestly and humbly before Him.

THE JOURNEY

Have you ever worried that you might not really be a Christian?

Guilt, guilt, and more guilt. Arguing with other believers and not having love . . . guilt. Messing up and sometimes giving into sin . . . more guilt. This describes the feelings of those to whom John was writing. John knew these type of feelings well, for he had been there himself. He had a strong personality and had sometimes been unkind toward others. As a matter of fact, Jesus even nicknamed him "son of thunder"! In spite of this, however, Jesus was able to change John's life for the good.

John knew the believers to whom he was writing needed encouragement. They needed to be challenged to be honest before God. In so doing, they would improve not only their relationship with God, but also their relationships with one another. They would be able to withstand Satan and the doubts he placed in their minds concerning their salvation.

John pulled out his parchment and set to writing. "What I am writing to you concerns Jesus who is the Word of Life. He is someone I have not only heard and seen with my eyes, but have actually touched, personally experienced, and know to be true." John was older now, and those to whom he was writing had never had the opportunity to see the things John had seen with his own eyes. Because John was an apostle and one of Jesus' original disciples, he could write about these things with authority.

Confess means to agree with God. When you confess your sins, you are agreeing with God (who knows exactly what you've done) that you did something wrong. You can then ask forgiveness.

"If we claim to be without sin, we are only fooling ourselves. However, if we admit our sin to God, He is faithful and just and He will forgive us. Not only will He forgive us, but He will also cleanse us and purify our lives from all unrighteousness!" This was a promise he had tried and knew to be true.

John knew the importance of believing God and doing what God says, for this shows what a person really believes. "We know that we have come to know Him if we obey His commands," John wrote. He then told how true believers don't have their lives ruled by hate, but rather they confess their wrong attitudes and ask God to forgive them. They don't continually practice sin, although they may sin and make mistakes. They don't love the world or live for its treasures, but instead love Jesus and aren't ashamed to tell others about Him. A perfect life is not an indicator of a true believer, for no one can be perfect. Rather, a life that seeks God and desires to live for Him—that is a true test that a person belongs to God's family.

"How great is God's love that He heaps upon us, by allowing us to be called His children! The Father sent the Son to be the Savior of the world. We can stand confident in this and know that we live in Him and that He lives in us. We know this by the Spirit He has given us."

CLIMBING ONWARD

Find I John 2:6. What does it say? This is where the rubber meets the road!

Skill Time

As we strive to walk as Jesus did, we will mess up and do wrong things—much like John did. When we fail we often feel guilty and begin to hide from God. We begin to doubt our salvation (much to Satan's pleasure). The more Satan accuses us, the more guilty we feel. Rather than fall into this trap, we need to stand on the promises of God. Look up I John 1:9 and read it for yourself (don't read on, look it up!). Mark this verse. Now, read it aloud and say your name in the place of the words we and us. Is there anything you need to confess to God right now? Take the time to do it. Also, commit this verse to memory and use it when Satan tries to lay a guilt trip on you or get you to doubt your salvation.

ALL THIS IS MINE?

TAKEN FROM I JOHN 4—5

GETTING READY

As you finish your journey through I John, ask the Lord to help you become more sure of your salvation. Give Him permission to work in your life so you might be able to reflect His love to others.

THE JOURNEY

Have you ever wondered why loving others is so important to God?

John sat staring at the parchment, his heart full of love for the believers to whom he was writing. Already he had encouraged those who were doubting their salvation. Now, he would go a step further and reassure them of all the treasures they had because of God's love. Once they understood this, they would be able to return that love to God by loving one another.

John started by defining what God's love is like. "This is love," John wrote, "not that we loved God, but that God loved us and sent His Son as a sacrifice for our sins." God's love didn't depend upon what others did.

His love was a love of action and giving—to those who didn't deserve it. God gave the very best He had for the very worst of us.

John continued, "God's love casts away all our fears and allows us to grow. His love helps change our desires so we don't practice sin. Because of God's love, we are able to ask for things and know that He hears us. His love keeps us safe so the evil one (Satan) can't harm us. The world is under Satan's power, but we are children of God and belong to His family. This is all because of God's love and what He did for us through Jesus."

John knew the believers were familiar with this, yet they needed to be reminded. It was one thing to know and another, thing to put it into practice. "Dear friends," John challenged, "let us love one another for love comes from God. Whoever does not love must not know God, because the very nature of God is love. Since God (who is so mighty) loved us (who are so sinful), we have little choice but to love one another. In so

> Love is not a feeling—it is an action. It is looking out for the highest interest of others. That is what God does for us. That is what He expects us to do for others.

doing, we are obeying His commands and expressing love back to Him. Real love is to obey His commands."

The believers who didn't express God's love were in danger of drifting away from Him. Perhaps they were too busy or too tired to love one another. Or, perhaps they had their needs met in God's love yet didn't look beyond themselves and their own wants. John closed his letter with a simple sentence that would stand as a challenge for all time. "My dear children," John warned, "keep yourselves from idols, and from anything that would keep you from returning God's love."

CLIMBING ONWARD

Look up I John 4:19-21. Why do we love? Why is loving others so important? (HINT: two reasons—one found in verse 20, and one in verse 21.)

DANGER AHEAD

Idols are not just statues that sit on a shelf. Idols are anything that takes the place of God or of what God commands us to do. They involve loving things more than we love God. There will be times in your life when you will be tempted to trade all the treasures you have in God's love for things that can't even come close. Don't give in. Rather, guard your heart and respond to God's love with love for Him. Show Him love by doing what He commands.

GETTING YOUR BEARINGS:
THE BOOK OF JUDE

The Book of Jude was written eighteen years after the book of James and almost twenty–seven years before the books of I, II, and III John. In our Bibles, however, we find it coming after the books of I, II, III John. (Remember, the New Testament is not put together in the order it was written!)

Jude, like James, was a half brother of Jesus. He was a half brother because he shared only the same mother with Jesus. Jude and James both had Joseph as their father, but Jesus was born of the Holy Spirit.

Jude, like James, did not believe in Jesus as the Savior when Jesus was still alive. It wasn't until after the Resurrection that Jude came to realize that the words Jesus said about Himself were true. It was at that point that Jude became a believer in Christ.

Jude wrote his letter to Jewish Christians, although it applies to all Christians. In it, Jude warned against those who come into the church and try to lead believers away from their faith in Jesus.

As you journey through Jude, notice what Jude had to say about false believers. Also, be encouraged by the final note of victory all believers share in Jesus!

WATCH IT!

TAKEN FROM JUDE VERSES 1-23

GETTING READY

Spend time thanking God for His truth and the ability you have to know Him. Ask Him to keep you from the influences of others who might try to pull you away from your faith in Him.

THE JOURNEY

Have you ever wondered how some people get pulled into false religions and cults?

Jude wadded up his parchment and started over. As much as he tried, he could not write a joyous letter celebrating salvation. It seemed God was burdening him with a different message of great importance, and he knew he must write what God placed upon his heart.

"Dear friends, although I wanted to write about the salvation we share, I felt God wanted me to write something different. It is a word of warning about certain impostors who have slipped in among you," Jude wrote. The impostors he described were men who had joined up with the believers, pretending to be one of them when actually they were enemies. "These godless men distort the meaning of God's grace by making it into an opportunity to sin. Not only that, they deny Jesus Christ our Lord."

Jude continued, describing how these people behave and the judgment that is coming upon them. He compared their actions to those of three men in the Old Testament. "Woe to them for they have created their own ways of worship and hate those who are righteous, much like Cain. They pretend to serve God while encouraging others to sin so they might gain from it, much like Balaam. They rebel against God's authority by standing against those God puts in charge, much like Korah led a revolt against God's chosen leaders—Moses and Aaron. Their end is only destruction."

Jude described the impostors as clouds without rain—they promised one thing but didn't deliver and were soon gone, just like a cloud driven by the wind. Such people were like uprooted autumn trees that bore no fruit. They bore no spiritual fruit and had no spiritual foundation. No fruit and no foundation made them as good as dead!

Jude then turned from a warning to a challenge—a challenge to resist being taken in by such impostors. "Dear friends, build yourselves up by growing in your knowledge of the faith." By "the faith," Jude meant the true teachings they had from the apostles, which were now recorded in Scripture. The more they built themselves up in

Jude also compared impostors to shooting stars, which gave little light and had no direction. Unlike the fixed stars by which sailors navigated their boats, those who plotted their course by shooting stars would only be led off course and be lost.

Scripture, the more they would be able to stand against falsehood. "Pray in the Holy Spirit and keep yourself in God's love," he instructed. This meant they were to continue depending upon the Holy Spirit in all areas of their spiritual life and to grow in their love for God even more. The believers were to keep their eyes focused upon Jesus who was their hope.

Jude's final words seemed to sum up everything. "Stand and fight for the faith," he wrote. By living and fighting for the truth, the believers would be fighting against impostors and false teachings.

CLIMBING ONWARD

Find Jude 3 in your Bible. (NOTE: Since Jude is only one chapter long, the number 3 refers to the verse). The word *contend* means to do battle for; to defend. Skip down to verses 17, 20, 21. According to these verses, how is this to be done?

DANGER AHEAD

People who are enemies of the Gospel don't wear big signs stating that fact. Rather, they work undercover, trying to win the favor of others and then leading them astray. Jesus warned about such people. Today, we have a term for such groups of people. They are called "cults." These cults usually have a leader who everyone thinks is great or wise. The leaders are usually regular people like you or me. Sometimes they may claim to have a word from God, or have special abilities. They often try to separate you from your family, or they may have peculiar rules to follow. Watch out for cults. Take the steps Jude instructed of building, praying, keeping, and looking to Jesus. These will keep your focus and head in the right place.

VICTORY! YES!

TAKEN FROM JUDE VERSES 24-25

GETTING READY

Spend a few minutes praising God for His power and strength. Thank Him that He is in control and sees and knows everything. Thank Him that He has the final word on things.

THE JOURNEY

Have you ever been in a situation where all you could do was try your best and hope it all worked out?

Build yourself up in the faith; pray in the Holy Spirit; keep yourself in the love of God; and look to Jesus. Jude knew these were all important things to do when watching out for false teachers and impostors. They were things believers needed to do for themselves.

With a sigh of great relief, Jude's thoughts soared upward as he recalled the One who really gives the victory. This victory is not just in protection against impostors, but in all areas of the believer's life!

"Praise be to Jesus who is able to keep you from falling." Jude's pen seemed to explode across the page in a final note of triumph. He knew believers would stumble and fall. They would make mistakes and mess up, but God was still in control. Jesus was faithful and more than able to keep the souls of believers and protect those who had given their lives to Him.

"Jesus will not only keep you from falling," Jude wrote, "but He will present you before God's glorious presence blameless, without fault, and with great joy!" There could be no greater words of encouragement and confidence. Victory and success did not lie in the hands of each believer; victory and success rested in the hands of Jesus. Believers did not have to just hope everything would work out; they could know it would.

These were Jude's closing words. He ended his letter on a note of celebration and victory: "To the only God our Savior, be glory, majesty, power and authority through Jesus Christ our Lord—both now, and forevermore! Amen."

Find Jude 24-25 in your Bible. What does it say? What is the result of Jesus keeping us from falling? (See verse 25.)

Skill Time

Here is another great verse to put in your memory bank! It is a reminder of victory through the hands of Someone who is far greater than we are—Jesus!

Take a piece of paper or note card and copy down Jude 24. On the back of the card, draw a picture of the things that often cause you to fall (attitudes, your relationships with others, etc.). Spend a few minutes giving these things over to God. Place this verse somewhere where you will see it every morning. For the next five days, read this verse while you are dressing, and remind yourself of the victory you have in Christ. Then, as you face your day and stumble into the things which tend to make you fall, remember the victory you have in Jesus and act accordingly.

Getting Your Bearings:
THE BOOK OF REVELATION

The Greek word for *revelation* comes from the Greek word, *apoka-lypsis* which means "unveiling; unwrapping; uncovering something that was hidden." The Book of Revelation centers around one thing, and one thing only—Jesus Christ. It reveals things about Jesus (such as Him being judge, redeemer, and triumphant king) as well as describes future events (such as the judgment of people, nations, and sin).

This book was written by the apostle John, who also wrote the Gospel of John and I, II, III John. As you may remember, in John's later life he lived in Ephesus and was one of the last remaining apostles alive. While John wrote the Book of Revelation, however, he was living on the island of Patmos (a type of prison-island), having been sentenced to live there by the emperor Domitian.

Domitian was an emperor who insisted that all people worship him, and he demanded to be called "Lord" and "God". Those who failed to do so were punished or put to death. John was on the island of Patmos because of his stand for Christ, refusing to worship the emperor.

As you journey through the Book of Revelation, hang in there. There are many things we don't understand and may never fully understand until we get to heaven. Those things are not the important things. Keep your focus on Jesus, who is the center and focus of this book. Don't get off on the little stuff concerning what and when certain things might happen. Instead, know that if God said they will happen, they will.

It is not the purpose of *Caution: Dangerous Devotions* to walk all the way through the Book of Revelation, for that alone would take a book this size! Instead, you will journey through sections of Revelation, getting a taste and feel for what it is all about.

THAT HITS CLOSE TO HOME

TAKEN FROM REVELATION 1—3

GETTING READY

Before you journey through God's Word today, stop and ask the Lord to speak to your heart. Ask Him to help you get a better picture of who He is, and who you are.

THE JOURNEY

What do you think Jesus is like in heaven? What do you think He desires from you?

John wrote his letter of the Revelation to seven churches in the province of Asia that were on a mail route. Look at a map to see Ephesus (not far from the island of Patmos). Going north, find Smyrna, then Pergamum where the route turns in a circle so it is now going south. The rest of the cities followed—Thyatira, Sardis, Philadelphia, and Laodicea.

These seven cities each had a church to whom John addressed a special part of his letter. As John's letter was passed along the mail route, each church read the whole letter, and gave special attention to the section specifically directed to them.

John began his letter of the Revelation by focusing his readers on the person of Jesus. "To Jesus who loves us and has freed us from our sins by His blood, to Him be glory and power for ever and ever!" Next John described how he was on the island of Patmos when God gave him this vision, telling John what to write. John began with words Jesus said about Himself, then tried to describe all that Jesus allowed him to see in his vision. "I am the Alpha and the Omega—the beginning and the end of things," Jesus said. "I am who is, who was, and who is to come. I am the Almighty."

As John wrote to each church what Jesus told him, he noticed that each description of Jesus about Himself fit a specific need that particular church had.

The first church was in Ephesus. According to the Lord, Ephesus had one problem: the believers didn't have the right priorities in their life and had left their first love. It wasn't that they had lost their love, but rather that they had left it. Jesus described Himself to these believers as the one who empowers the churches and the one who makes His dwelling among them. He is the powerful one; the protector, and the provider. They needed to remember this, repent from their wrongdoing, and re-kindle their love for Him.

The next church was in Smyrna. *Smyrna* comes from the Greek word *myrrh* and is a picture of suffering. In this city, emperor worship was required. Those who didn't worship the emperor faced great persecution. Jesus had nothing bad to say about this small church. Rather, He encouraged them to endure their persecution even if it led to death. He reassured them that He is the Alpha and Omega, and the conqueror of death. (This church still exists and is in today's city of Izmir, Turkey.)

The church of Pergamum didn't receive a good report. At first Jesus praised them for remaining true to His name and staying with the faith. Yet, in spite of this, they didn't move onward. They allowed the teaching and following of false teachers. Jesus described Himself as a judge who would judge their actions with the two-edged sword (the Word of God) coming from His mouth.

Jesus said the church at Thyatira was improving but still tolerating sin. He described Himself to them as the holy Son of God, full of purity. He described Himself as looking at them with laser-beam eyes to see what's inside. Instead of the danger coming from outside sources, the church of Thyatira was rotting from the inside! This church was gone by the end of the second century.

The next church, Sardis, was accused of being dead. Once they were a great church, but no more. Little by little the church began to change, until finally it was a group of people playing church. They did not have God's Spirit living in them. Jesus described Himself as the one who has and gives the Holy Spirit, and who gives power and life.

Philadelphia was the next church mentioned. Of this church Jesus said only good things. Philadelphia was used as a missionary church and a gateway to spreading the Gospel in the East. Jesus said even though they had little strength, they kept His word and did not deny Him. They were not a perfect church, but they were pleasing to God. Jesus described Himself as the one who is holy (set apart) and true, and the one who has the keys and rewards of heaven.

The last city on the mail route, Laodicea, had its water piped in from a nearby city. By the time the water reached them, it was lukewarm and unappetizing to drink. Jesus used a description these people would fully understand. He accused them of being lukewarm. He stated He would spit them out of His mouth. These believers felt they needed nothing and were doing fine when actually they were spiritually poor, blind, and naked in the Lord's eyes. To them, Jesus described Himself as being the faithful and true witness; the Amen. Everything He says is always true—including His description of them and what He desired.

CLIMBING ONWARD

Read Revelation 1:3. What does it say? How should you respond?

Skill Time

If your walk with Jesus could be described by one of these churches, which one best describes you? Review the examples of the churches. When you find one best describing you, read what Jesus has to say about Himself and His character. Strive to live that way because of who Jesus is.

THE REASON

TAKEN FROM REVELATION 4—7

GETTING READY

Pray, asking God to help you gain a better understanding of Jesus' glory and the worship that is due Him. Ask Him to help you appreciate all the more who He is and what He has done.

THE JOURNEY

Have you ever wondered why Jesus is waiting so long to come back?

The scene John saw in heaven was glorious! John was allowed to catch a glimpse of Jesus' glory in heaven and the things that are to come. Because our minds and eyes have never looked upon something so awesome, we have a hard time understanding the things John saw!

John began by describing a throne in heaven. The one who sat there had the appearance of a clear jasper stone, much like a brilliant diamond, and a carnelian (red ruby). Interestingly, the jasper and carnelian stone were the first and the last of the twelve gemstones worn across the high priest's robe. The throne looked beautiful beyond all comparison and had a rainbow, much like a green emerald, encircling it.

Around the throne were twenty-four lesser thrones where twenty-four elders sat. They wore crowns that were not like that of a king, but rather crowns that were rewarded to runners who finished as winners in the Greek games. We are not certain if these elders represent believers who have been rewarded in heaven or angels who have been given great responsibilities. Either way, the point is that they were worshiping God. John also saw flashes of lightning and rumblings and peals of thunder. God the Father sat on the throne, and the Holy Spirit was represented or symbolized by the seven lamp stands.

In front of the throne, John saw a sea of glass, clear as crystal. He also saw four living beings, which he compared to a lion, an ox, a man, and a flying eagle. Each had six wings and was covered with eyes. We do not fully understand about these beings, but it has been suggested they represent God's character. He is all–knowing and all–present (the eyes and wings). The lion represents His power and majesty. The ox shows His faithful work and patience. The man represents intelligence; the eagle, God's supreme rulership and authority.

The important thing is not what these beings were, but rather what they were doing. They were worshiping God as the Creator of the universe. The elders worshiped by laying their crowns before His throne.

The stage was set for Jesus. John saw Jesus as the Lamb of God, and heard those who were worshiping say, "Worthy is Jesus, for He was slain and He purchased with His blood men from every tribe, and tongue, and people, and nation. . . . To God who sits on the throne and to the Lamb be blessing, honor, and glory forever!"

John said he looked up and saw a great number of people, which no one could count. They were believers from every tribe, people, and nation, standing before Jesus in white robes. John continued, telling of the judgment that was to come upon the world in God's perfect timing.

When we reach that perfect time, Jesus will come back as He promised—suddenly and with great victory. Until that time, His Word must go forth so that people from every tribe, tongue, and nation will have a chance to be included in those who worship around God's throne.

CLIMBING ONWARD

Turn to Revelation 7:10. Notice what it says about salvation. Now, look up at verse 9. Who is singing this praise?

THINKING on your FEET

Will some people be in heaven because they heard about Jesus from you? Your faithfulness to share the Gospel and the way you live has an impact far greater than you will ever know! Live for God until Jesus returns.

JOURNEY ONWARD!

TAKEN FROM REVELATION 19—22

GETTING READY

As you finish your journey through the Book of Revelation, notice Jesus in all His glory, might, honor and power! He is the victor. He will come as promised; His timing is coming nearer.

THE JOURNEY

What do you think heaven will be like? Do you ever wonder if it will be boring?

"I saw heaven opened," John described, "and a white horse with one sitting upon it who is called faithful and true. In righteousness He will judge and wage war. His eyes are like flames of fire and He wears many crowns upon His head. He is clothed with a robe dipped in blood and He comes for final judgment and victory. His name is called the Word of God. All the armies of heaven were clothed in fine white robes and were following Him upon white horses. On His robe and on His thigh He bore the name KING OF KINGS, AND LORD OF LORDS."

John went on to describe Jesus coming back to earth. John wrote about the great judgments that would come and how Satan would be cast away into the lake of fire. The earth as we know it will pass away, but a new heaven and earth will be created—it will be much different and far better. We don't know what it will look like except that it will have no sea.

"I saw a New Jerusalem (representing the city of God) coming down out of heaven," John wrote, "and I heard the voice of an angel say 'Behold, God's dwelling place is among men. He will dwell among them and they will be His people. He will wipe away every tear from their eyes, and there will no longer be any death or sadness, crying, or pain, for all of these things have passed away.' " John heard the Lord say, "Behold, I am making all things new."

John went on to describe the New Jerusalem as coming down from heaven and having the glory of God. It was brilliant like gleaming precious stones. It had four sides with three gates on each. It was in the shape of a huge cube, being 1,400 miles long on each side, and 1,400 miles high! It was surrounded by a wall that was 216 feet thick! It looked like gold, only it was clear like glass! The wall surrounding the city had twelve foundation stones, and on them the names of the twelve apostles were written. The twelve gates were made of pearl.

What an awe-inspiring thought! In John 14:2, 3, Jesus said He goes to prepare a place for believers and will come again to receive them so that where He is, there they may be also. Could Jesus be referring to the New Jerusalem?

John noticed there was no temple in the New Jerusalem, and this was because the Lord God (the Almighty) and the Lamb (Jesus) are its temple. The city also had no sun or moon to shine upon it, for the glory of the Lord supplied it with blazing light.

In this new heavenly Jerusalem which comes down to the new earth, the curse of Adam and Eve will end. No healing will be necessary. God and the Lamb will dwell in the new city and God's throne will also be in it. Our highest joy and privilege will be to serve our Lord in eternity and rule with Him! We will see Him face to face, and His name will be on our foreheads, showing that we belong to Him!

John closed his letter with a charge that everything he had written about was true. "If anyone adds to these words, God will add to him the judgments that are written in this book," John stated, also giving a warning for those who take away from the words of this prophecy.

"Jesus, who has told us of these things says, 'Yes, I am coming quickly.' " As John pondered the awesome things he had seen and knew were coming, he knew eternal life would be far from boring! John closed his letter by breathing a prayer, "Amen. Come, Lord Jesus!"

CLIMBING ONWARD

Read Revelation 22:7. What does Jesus say to us? Who will be blessed?

Skill Time

Your relationship with God begins here and simply continues in heaven (the New Jerusalem). Continue on your journey with God. Even though you have arrived at the end of this book and have probably grown, there is still lots of ground ahead to cover! Look up Revelation 22:21. Never forget that we live by the grace of the Lord Jesus Christ. Keep your focus ever on Him.

A SPECIAL MESSAGE JUST FOR YOU!

The most important decision you will ever make in your life is the decision to accept or reject Jesus. Some people think they can get by without making this kind of decision, but that is not true. Jesus said if you don't make a decision to follow Him, you are actually making a decision to reject Him!

IN THE BIBLE WE LEARN THAT:

1. *We are all sinners* (Romans 3:23) and we cannot live up to God's standards of holiness. No matter how hard we try, we will always fall short. This creates a big problem, for it means no human can ever get to heaven by trying to live a good life. It also creates a problem, for God is righteous and He must punish sin.

2. *The wages of sin is death* (Romans 6:23). Just like death separates us from our loved ones, spiritual death separates us from the love of God. Those who have sin in their life cannot enter heaven, where God is.

3. *The gift of God is eternal life* (Romans 6:23). Because of God's great love and mercy (see John 3:16), He sent His Son, Jesus, to die on a cross and pay the penalty for our sins. It is a gift we did not earn or deserve.

4. *We must receive this gift* (John 1:12). Just like a gift is not ours until we accept it, we must choose to accept God's gift of eternal life in Jesus.

In John 14:6 we learn that there is only one way to have our sins forgiven so we can go to heaven. Jesus says He is the Way, the Truth, and the Life. No one comes to the Father except through Him.

We receive this gift by believing upon the Lord Jesus Christ. When we do this we become children of God and can belong to God's forever family!

HOW CAN YOU DO THIS?

You can simply pray to God, and tell Him what you desire. There are no special formula or words. God offers you the gift of salvation and is waiting for you to accept it.

1. Tell God you are sorry for your sins. (Sins are any wrong things you do, or the wrong attitudes you have, such as anger, pride, selfishness, etc.) Ask God to forgive you. Tell Him you want to become a part of His forever family.

2. Thank Jesus for dying on the cross for your sins and for taking your punishment. Ask Him to come into your life and make you the kind of person He wants you to be. Jesus said whoever comes to Him, He will give them eternal life.

You've now begun your journey with God. Just like newborn babies need to grow, you need to grow, too. You do this by reading your Bible, praying, going to church, and seeking to live the kind of life that pleases God.

Congratulations! You've just begun an exciting journey!